GOLDEN AGE S

Studies in European History

Series Editors: Richard Overy
John Breuilly
Peter Wilson

Golden Age Spain

Second edition

Henry Kamen

First published 2005 by
PALGRAVE MACMILLAN
Houndmills, Basingstoke, Hampshire RG21 6XS and
175 Fifth Avenue, New York, N. Y. 10010
Companies and representatives throughout the world

PALGRAVE MACMILLAN is the global academic imprint of the Palgrave
Macmillan division of St. Martin's Press, LLC and of Palgrave Macmillan Ltd.
Macmillan® is a registered trademark in the United States, United Kingdom
and other countries. Palgrave is a registered trademark in the European
Union and other countries.

ISBN 1–4039–3337–5

This book is printed on paper suitable for recycling and
made from fully managed and sustained forest sources.

A catalogue record for this book is available from the British Library.

A catalog record for this book is available from the Library of Congress

10   9   8   7   6   5   4   3   2   1
14 13 12 11 10 09 08 07 06 05

Printed in China

Contents

Editor's Preface

The main purpose of this new series of studies is to make available to teacher and student alike developments in a field of history that has become increasingly specialised with the sheer volume of new research and literature now produced. These studies are designed to present the 'state of the debate' on important themes and episodes in European history since the sixteenth century, presented in a clear and critical way by someone who is closely concerned himself with the debate in question.

The studies are not intended to be read as extended bibliographical essays, though each will contain a detailed guide to further reading which will lead students and the general reader quickly to key publications. Each book carries its own interpretation and conclusions, while locating the discussion firmly in the centre of the current issues as historians see them. It is intended that the series will introduce students to historical approaches which are in some cases very new and which, in the normal course of things, would take many years to filter down into the textbooks and school histories. I hope it will demonstrate some of the excitement historians, like scientists, feel as they work away in the vanguard of their subject. The series has an important contribution to make in publicising what it is that historians are doing and in making history more open and accessible. It is vital for history to communicate if it is to survive.

R. J. OVERY

A Note on References

References are cited throughout in brackets according to the numbering in the general bibliography, with page references where necessary indicated by a semi-colon after the bibliography number.

1 Introduction

Few Europeans have disagreed so much about their own country as Spaniards. The difference of opinion, centring both on culture and on politics, dates back to at least the eighteenth century and is still acute today. It affects the way that Spaniards look at their past and write about themselves, their history and their literature. In culture, traditionalists have tended to defend the glories of the medieval Reconquest, the solidity of peninsular Catholicism, the heroic expansion of empire and the triumph of the language of Cervantes, factors that made Spain uniquely different. Innovators and modernisers, by contrast, have criticised the country's separation from the western tradition of liberal thought and science. In politics, the traditionalists have defended the monarchy and the territorial unity of Spain, while their opponents have criticised monarchy and asserted the right of the provinces to be free of centralised control.

The very terms 'Golden Age' and 'Spain' have provoked disagreement. 'The nation', wrote the American historian W. H. Prescott in his history of the reign of Ferdinand and Isabella (1838), 'emerging from the sloth and licence of a barbarous age, seemed to prepare like a giant to run its course'. No sooner had he surveyed the reign than he concluded that the subsequent Habsburg epoch could not be termed a 'golden age', since in comparison it exhibited little more than 'the hectic brilliancy of decay'. Yet it was precisely this later period of 'decay', representing most of the centuries covered by the present short book, that later historians and experts on literature chose to describe as 'golden'. The clear contradiction shows that in reality the word 'golden' has never had any precise meaning. For those who lived in the sixteenth century it referred to an idealised period located in the past rather than their own time of troubles, and Cervantes in 1605 made his Don

1

Quixote yearn for 'those happy golden centuries' of a bygone age. Up to the eighteenth century, Spaniards identified the 'golden' epoch almost exclusively with the Catholic Monarchs. Literary critics in the period of the Enlightenment also judged that the cultural successes of the sixteenth and seventeenth centuries merited the title of 'golden', and their view has since passed into common use. Inevitably, what was 'golden' became identified with success, and 'what was not golden' with failure. This took on ideological hues that still remain with us: the gold of the Golden Age continues to be defended with unusual passion by many traditionalists.

The word 'Spain' continues to pose problems. In medieval times it could mean the entire peninsula and therefore included Portugal (the Portuguese poet Camões called Portugal and Spain 'the Spains'). For the period down to the year 1714, however, it is important to be aware that 'Spain' (like 'Germany' or 'Italy') was little more than a loose word covering a disunited variety of regions, cultures, governments and consciousnesses. Spaniards used it when talking about their country to foreigners; among themselves, they reverted to specific regional names. The word did not in the Habsburg period feature in the official list of titles of the 'king of Spain', who might use it simply for brevity. Because it described no specific political unit it could command the formal loyalty of provinces (such as the Basque country) that otherwise ruled themselves according to their own institutions and customs. Spain's diversity was in a sense also its strength. Thanks to its dominant role in the peninsula, however, Castile took over much of the identity of 'Spain', with consequences that continue to affect very profoundly the culture and politics of today. In the same way, there was no one 'Spanish' language. Though Castilian was the principal Spanish language, many Spaniards – over a quarter of the whole population, if to the Catalans and Portuguese we add a high proportion of Galicians, Basques and Moriscos – did not normally converse in 'Spanish' but in their own regional speech. The imprecision of what is meant by 'Spain' has important consequences for students trying to understand its history and culture. During the sixteenth and seventeenth centuries when the king made laws he normally made them not for 'Spain' but for 'Castile'; when decrees mentioned 'these realms' the reference was usually to the realms of Castile and León only. The laws had no force in the Crown of Aragon or the Basque provinces, unless special measures were taken by the king of Spain and the governments in those areas. It is a consideration that should be kept in mind when using this book.

Since the first edition came out (1988) much new research has emerged. An attempt has been made to mention the most relevant items in English, the language of most users of this text. Out of the very large number of studies published in Spanish, only a few are mentioned, but items cited in English will normally contain references to further studies in Spanish and other languages. The contribution made by non-Spaniards to the study of things Spanish is so outstanding as to require little apology. Prescott, Merriman and H.C. Lea over a century ago pioneered the important researches made by English-language scholars [1], and half a century ago it was the turn of French experts such as Fernand Braudel [2] and Pierre Vilar [3]. Students of history are able to choose from numerous English-language textbooks, among them my own [4]. There are good modern texts by John Lynch [5] and Stanley Payne [6], of which the latter is conveniently available as an e-book [7].

Attention to regional themes has in recent decades received enormous stimulus from Spain's autonomous governments, which have funded research schemes that emphasise the historic character of the relevant province. As a result, valuable multi-volume histories have been published of all the provincial autonomies, including Castile itself. The regional approach has the virtue of emphasising traditions and characteristics – in Catalonia and in Galicia, for example – that the Franco dictatorship (1939–75) played down, though it also runs the risk of ignoring some of the great unifying factors in Iberian history. In the present outline, due attention will be given to regional issues and aspects of the monarchy outside the peninsula, but more special emphasis will be placed on factors linking Spain to European trends, since all too often the country is treated as though it were alien to the main features of western civilisation.

The intention here is to offer a short and balanced guide to the current state of scholarship, with an emphasis on recent bibliography and central questions that are the subject of discussion and debate. At a time when many students find it more convenient to consult materials in their computers than to attend formal classes, several websites in English offer help though the information they give varies in quality. The model for a web page directed to university students is assuredly that on the Spanish Empire run by Prof J. B. Owens of the University of Idaho [8], which contains recent bibliography and offers advice on writing papers.

In the few cases where money values are given, no attempt is made to give modern equivalents. The capitalised form 'Crown of Aragon' is used to refer to the associated realms of Catalonia, Valencia and Aragon; the form 'kingdom of Aragon' is used for the last-mentioned realm.

2 Absolute Monarchy in Spain

Was there an 'absolute' monarchy in Early Modern Spain? What were the 'crown', the 'monarchy' and the 'state'? How did the crown enforce its authority? Modifying state power: provincial and urban authority. How did the crown pay its way? Was there opposition to and popular protest against the government? What changes came with Bourbon power?

Between 1450 and 1714 Spain underwent a more extensive political evolution than probably any other west European state of its time. In the late fifteenth century the Spanish realms (one of them Muslim) were a confused collection of jurisdictions with wholly separate identities; by the early eighteenth century there remained only one authority, the crown of 'Spain'. Though the transformation appeared to be fundamental, it left untouched basic elements of society, culture and religion that continued to preserve their character without much change over subsequent centuries.

Was there an 'absolute' monarchy in Early Modern Spain? Traditionally, historians pointed to the growth of royal authority as the most notable political fact, but later studies have looked more closely at what this really involved [9]. After the anarchy of the civil wars in Castile and Catalonia in the late fifteenth century, the reign of Ferdinand and Isabella (1474–1516) seemed to initiate the birth of a modern state. The rulers presided over the union of their crowns, the defeat of the Muslims of Granada, the expulsion of the Jews, the discovery of the New World, and the beginnings of Spanish power in southern Italy, the North African coast and the Atlantic (the Canary Islands). The successes invited admiration and subsequent mythification. 'Our Spain never achieved such perfection as in those times',

5

wrote González de Cellorigo in 1600. Ferdinand 'began the greatness of this immense monarchy', Fernández de Navarrete wrote at the same period. Over three centuries later, a conservative tradition, at its most influential under the Franco regime, went so far as to adopt as its emblem the royal device of Isabella, the 'yoke and arrows'. Anglo-Saxon historians praised the Spanish rulers as 'new monarchs', drawing parallels between them and the dynasties of other emergent nation states such as England and France.

More recently, historians [10] have managed to distance themselves from the old myths, which continue to survive because nationalist and religious ideologies in Spain still nurture them. In perspective, the reigns of the 'Catholic Monarchs' (a title granted to Ferdinand and Isabella by the pope in 1496) coincided with important innovations that justify the admiration of later generations, but not the belief that they created a new state. They certainly did not unite Spain (see later), nor did they add substantially to royal power, nor did they reform the Church (on this, see Chapter 5). Isabella, moreover, played little part in the formation of the Spanish Empire. She helped to finance Columbus, but when she died in 1504 Hernan Cortés had only just landed in America. The queen's testament did not even mention the existence of the New World and claimed no sovereignty over Naples [11].

Between the fifteenth and eighteenth centuries the monarchy changed its character substantially. Under Ferdinand and Isabella it was an exclusively Mediterranean entity. Under the Habsburg dynasty (1516–1700) it accepted an extensive European and world perspective. Under the first Bourbon (1700–46) it reverted again to a largely Mediterranean role, with a secondary function in the New World. Through all these vicissitudes the crown managed to augment its authority, though this did not necessarily imply an increase in power. The different aspects of power under the Catholic Monarchs and their successors can be approached through the three realities of 'crown', 'monarchy' and 'state'.

What were the 'crown', the 'monarchy' and the 'state'? The power of the 'crown' was personal and also symbolic, but if there were any pretensions to absolute power they could be found only in Castile. As early as the fourteenth century, the king of Castile had claimed 'absolute power', and in 1439 Juan II stated that 'so great is the king's right to power, that all laws and all rights are subject to him, and his authority is not from men but from God, whose place he occupies in temporal matters'. The claims to 'absolute power' were repeated under the Catholic Monarchs, and Isabella used the phrase seven times in her testament. As a result, some historians used to claim that the regime of Ferdinand and Isabella was 'absolutist', and even extended the description to later reigns (especially that of Philip II). The view is now seen to be completely untenable. The kings of Castile were in reality an exception among the monarchies of Western Europe. They consciously rejected many of the symbols of power used by monarchies outside the peninsula [12]. They did not consider their office sacred, did not claim (like the rulers of France and England) any power to heal the sick, and enjoyed no special rituals at the time of their birth or crowning or death [13]. The imagery of magical royal power, common in other monarchies, was notably absent in Spain. The rulers of Castile from Isabella to Philip II and beyond evolved no coronation ceremony and no cult of personality. Most even fought shy of the title 'Majesty': Isabella was simply 'Highness' and Philip II from 1586 ordered that his ministers and officials address him only as 'Sir'.

In practice, the reality or otherwise of absolutism can probably be best measured by the position of the crown relative to the law of the realm. Was the crown in a position to make law without the need to obtain consent? Was it able to by-pass the law? The evidence shows that law-making was at best a part-time activity of kings (Philip II made an average of eighteen laws a year, Philip IV about eight); and when we consider the ordinary and daily restrictions on royal authority the concept of absolutism seems to be little more than hot air. Neither Isabella nor Philip II nor any other Spanish ruler expressed an aspiration to be 'absolute'. In addition, few if any of the laws passed by the government were ever observed. All Spanish legists accepted certain practical limits to crown power, for instance that the king was still subject to divine law, or that only the king in person could act extra-legally but that he could not oblige the state, itself created by law, to break the law [14]. It is remarkable above all that political philosophy in Spain was notably anti-absolutist, especially when directed against foreign rulers and their theorists. Particularly around the year 1600, Jesuit thinkers such as Juan de Mariana and Francisco Suárez backed (with the crown's approval) ideas in favour of limiting kingly power. Tyrants, they wrote, can be deposed and even assassinated. Their works were bitterly denounced, and even burnt publicly, outside Spain; inside the country, there was no objection.

The word 'monarchy' meant of course the system of kingly rule, but for Spaniards it also meant the conglomerate of territories attached to the crown. The Spanish 'monarchy' was an association of multiple kingdoms like the original union of the Crown of Castile and the Crown of Aragon in the persons of Ferdinand and Isabella, in which each state functioned separately but under the aegis of a single crown. The dynastic principle was fundamental. 'All past monarchies began in violence and force of arms', wrote Gregorio López Madera in his *Excellences of the Monarchy of Spain* (1597), 'only that of Spain has had just beginnings, great part of it coming together by succession'. When Ferdinand was recognised as king of Naples in 1504, so bringing to an end the wars in southern Italy, the crown was deemed to be his personally; and by no means was Naples subjected to Spain. In the same way, Ferdinand claimed to be king of Navarre in 1512 by dynastic right; the kingdom that he occupied remained independent of but associated with Spain. The most decisive contribution to the creation of the 'monarchy' occurred when Charles of Burgundy succeeded in 1516 to the thrones of Castile and Aragon, bringing with him as part of his inheritance the states of the old duchy of Burgundy. Dynastic right was also the fundamental issue that led to the occupation of Portugal much later in 1580 by Philip II. Portugal too remained independent of Spain. Over and beyond the associated and independent states of the 'monarchy', Spain during these years built up control of other territories that contemporaries came to look upon as an 'empire' (see Chapter 3).

The various realms associated with early modern Spain retained their complete independence in government, laws, coinage and armed forces (there were, for example, autonomous parliaments in the Netherlands, Naples and Sicily) and were joined together only by obedience to a common sovereign. The French historian Pierre Chaunu in 1970 referred to this as a multiple monarchy or 'dynastic Grand Alliance of the seventeen crowns', and was among the first to emphasise the complex nature of an empire bound together by dynastic right. British historians have recently recognised that this system of 'multiple kingdoms' could also be identified in other parts of Europe, such as the British Isles [15]. Under Charles V, therefore, Castile came to accept its part in a community of nations. Each state in the association subject to the crown had different principles of government. Some, like the Basque provinces in the peninsula, were fully independent republics which did not even recognise the crown of Spain but accepted its ruler as their 'lord'. In the Crown of Aragon, the kings had to rule through a system of agreements (or 'pacts') with their elites. Everywhere in the 'monarchy' – Navarre, Naples and the Netherlands – traditional institutions restricted royal claims, and even in Castile a mediaeval tradition of consultation with the Cortes was affirmed during the Comunidades (1520) and in the 1620s during the opposition to Olivares' regime.

The 'state' meant administrative power. Since the development of royal authority in late fifteenth and early sixteenth century Spain took place primarily in Castile, and other realms of the peninsular monarchy remained immune to formal change, historians who discuss the 'state' have tended to concentrate on Castile. Ferdinand and Isabella did not, as we once believed, innovate significantly. Rather, they adapted traditional institutions and built up political alliances (above all with urban elites, nobles and the Church). As a result, while leaving the structure of power undisturbed they were astonishingly successful in getting various interests (in both Castile and Aragon) to respect their authority. Efficient government required that there be rules ('law') and finance ('taxes'). The decrees (*pragmáticas*) of the Catholic Monarchs and their successors were collected into 'codes' and became the basis of Castilian legislation. This meant, however, that the Castilian Cortes soon lost its function as a law-initiating body, despite repeated protests. In a strictly legal sense, the crown in Castile came to be seen as the source of law and therefore as 'sovereign'.

Nevertheless, there was little hope of augmenting royal power significantly in a land where there were serious day-to-day limits on crown authority. It is a vital aspect that is often ignored. Throughout the early modern period, in Castile the bulk of jurisdictions (i.e. rights of control over taxes and justice) was in the hands of the aristocracy and the Church. In Salamanca province, for example, two-thirds of territory and population were not controlled by the king in matters of finance and law and order. The situation was similar in much of the peninsula. In the kingdom of Aragon the crown

9

exercised jurisdiction over only 42 per cent of towns, in the realm of Valencia over only 25 per cent. Moreover, throughout Spain (including Castile) most cities and communities continued to enjoy traditional rights, known as '*fueros*', which protected them from outside authorities such as the king.

The '*fueros*' were particularly important in non-Castilian realms such as the Crown of Aragon, where constitutional bodies guarded them zealously and every unacceptable action or decree of the king was immediately judged to be an 'anti-fuero' and therefore illegal. A further defence, available in Castile but also used in America, was the idea that laws be 'obeyed but not put into effect'. For example, in 1527 a '*fuero*' of Vizcaya stated that any royal command 'that is or may be against the laws or fueros, be obeyed but not put into effect'. This usage (the '*pase foral*') was common in the Basque countries, illustrating the preference for compromise over conflict. The consequence was that the seemingly great power of the king was cushioned in practice, and it is difficult to identify any wholly 'absolute' actions by the crown in early modern Spain. In any case, every sensible monarch liked to be seen to be consulting rather than browbeating. Isabella never ceased to maintain that she was absolute, yet took care to pass all her laws inside the Castilian Cortes rather than out of it. Charles V granted to the Cortes of Castile in 1525 the right to have a permanent standing committee (*Diputación*) along the lines of those existing in the Crown of Aragon. Even Philip II, at a period when he was racked by severe illness, opted in 1592 to make the long journey to attend the Cortes that pacified Aragon after the troubles provoked by Antonio Pérez, and did not touch the Aragonese 'fueros'.

How did the crown enforce its authority? Royal power would have been quite hollow had no administrative infrastructure (the 'state') evolved to support it. Forty years ago [16] Vicens Vives outlined some problems of the emergent state bureaucracy, and Maravall in subsequent studies [17] showed how the evolution of state theory and administration in Spain was closely connected to developments in Europe. Bureaucracy was very slow to develop, and down to the early Habsburg period the 'state', as in mediaeval times, consisted of the crown and its immediate officials. Isabella administered her realm in a mediaeval and astonishingly popular fashion simply by travelling around and taking her officials with her.

Practical requirements soon demanded that more officials be created and that they become sedentary. Institutions and personnel began to develop: law courts (*chancillerías*), councils, secretaries of state [18]. By the reign of Philip II secretaries played a key role in coordinating government, and under Philip V they developed into ministerial heads of department. Of the councils that derived from late mediaeval models the most important was the Council of Castile, not only because it oversaw government of the largest of the Spanish realms but also because it was the highest legal body in the monarchy. From 1480 the Catholic Monarchs enforced existing rules about the legal qualifications and training required by its members. The bureaucratic demands of the state stimulated the study of law at university. At Salamanca and Alcalá canon and civil law were the preferred subjects, matriculations in law at the former during the seventeenth century outnumbering those in theology by twenty to one [19]. The contemporary Diego Hurtado de Mendoza observed that 'the Catholic Monarchs placed the administration of justice and public affairs into the hands of *letrados*' (law graduates).

No innovation in itself, the practice of appointing *letrados* as administrators became generalised: not only the courts and councils were staffed by them, but as many as half the *corregidores* of the sixteenth century were also *letrados*. The lawyers became in effect the new administrative class [20], and since they were almost without exception already of noble (*hidalgo*) rank their rise brought about few status conflicts with the established nobility (unlike France, where prolonged clashes of status took place). Moreover, from the mid-sixteenth century those with doctoral degrees from the principal Castilian and Aragonese universities were granted automatic noble status. It is worth noting that the lawyers were trained either in canon or in civil law or in both, making them eligible for office in both Church and state. Spain was in the probably unique position of having a unitary civil service, with clergy eligible for senior offices of state (many served as viceroys) and laymen eligible for Church posts (some early inquisitors were laymen). Unlike the bureaucracy of the French crown, the *letrado* hierarchy was not venal, that is, their posts were not as a rule bought or sold; this tended to make for greater efficiency and – even more important from the crown's point of view – helped to keep the posts under royal control. Entrenched in the administration, many *letrados* of fairly humble origin went on to found great dynasties of servants of the crown [21]. This by no means meant that the traditional nobility were deprived of their role in government; they still dominated some councils, notably the Council of State, and enjoyed a near monopoly of the major offices of state (viceroys, ambassadors).

The ordering of government and the growth of bureaucracy soon made it desirable to have an administrative centre. Until the mid-sixteenth century, the crown conducted most of its business from Valladolid, where the first two Habsburg rulers were proclaimed king and where an archive for state papers was established. Eventually in 1561 Philip II chose to fix his government at Madrid, since the town was in easy reach of his chain of residences. This (despite a common misapprehension) did not make Madrid into the capital of Spain, for the country was not yet a centralised state; but it confirmed the town as the seat of government and of the royal court. Madrid did not become capital of a united Spain until the Bourbon era. Though bureaucracy began to develop from the end of the fifteenth century, state power in Castile did not perceptibly increase. This was because the crown, when building up a body of reliable servants, used them generally not to interfere with or change institutions but to collaborate with them. We can see this in action both in the centre, with ministers of state, and in the provinces, with the key post of *corregidor* (or city governor). Corregidors were local officials of late-mediaeval origin, who kept the crown in touch with the great cities. They existed only in some parts of Castile, numbered no more than sixty by the end of the sixteenth century, and received their salaries from the city they served [22]. They cannot therefore be regarded as agents of royal power. Though there was a brief reaction against them during the Comunidades (1520–21), they continued to function satisfactorily throughout the Habsburg period. The new post of provincial intendant, introduced in 1711 [23], was based explicitly on them but with the major difference that the intendant had more extensive powers, and was an agent of centralised state government.

At the centre of government the possibility that the office of chief minister, made important by the absence of Charles V and the consequent concentration of authority in the hands of administrators such as Los Cobos [24], might develop into a permanent feature, disappeared with the resolve of Philip II to be his own chief minister. Under this strong king there were several powerful men of state, such as Antonio Pérez [25] and Juan de Idiáquez, but no significant increase in their functions. After Philip's death his weaker successors tended to put more authority in the hands of ministers who were known as *validos* [26], but these too did not implement any institutional change, and the only one with a coherent policy, Olivares [30], failed completely to achieve any of his declared aims. Under Olivares' successor the duke of Lerma [27], the *valido* made many important decisions but considerable initiative returned to the traditional system of councils [28], and the same process occurred under the *validos* of the time of Charles II. Not until the reign of Philip V did a profound revolution take place in the conduct of central government.

Historical biography offers a useful way of understanding how individuals shaped the course of events. Though it is invariably more interesting to approach the past through the actions of the people who were in charge, whether kings (and queens) or ministers, there is also a risk of exaggerating their roles. For some scholars, such as Fernand Braudel [2], the role and impact of the king or minister is much less than we might think, and it is the overall structure of power that usually dominates. Others, however, insist that the king as agent exercises decisive power and should be held responsible for all actions of his government [29]. The use of moral judgements in history has its attractions, since it gives us the satisfaction of identifying the person responsible for alleged crimes. Most historians, nevertheless, avoid acting as judge or jury. In early modern times, it can be argued, the power (and therefore responsibility) of both kings and ministers was always limited, and most political leaders (the outstanding case is Olivares) failed to achieve their objectives [30]. Some rulers, notably Isabella the Catholic and Philip II, worked hard at their job. Others, like Charles II and Philip V, had others do the work for them. The Habsburgs were by no means inept, and a fairly convincing attempt has been made to present Philip IV as a conscientious head of government [31]. However, ideological fashions tend to determine what textbooks say, and the rulers of Spain have always suffered fluctuating reputations within their own country.

Modifying state power: provincial and urban authority. What we have called the 'state' was still at an early stage of its growth. It is a fact that should warn us not to pay excessive attention to the role of the

13

crown, for royal control was by no means the most typical type of government. Pre-industrial Europe was largely self-governing, with highly localised structures, a simple fact which explains for example the ability of Spain to rule itself through the long years of Charles V's absences. What were these traditional structures? At the upper level, each realm of Spain had its own assembly, ranging from territories with traditional assemblies or Cortes (Castile, Crown of Aragon, Navarre) [32] to those with elective bodies (the Junta General of Vizcaya) [33]. The crown's representative had the right to be present at these meetings, as he was also entitled to be present at all formal assemblies of the Church; but it was rare for the crown to interfere in the process of decision-making. The elite was also left largely undisturbed in control of the government of the great cities, a control made even more secure by the crown's practice – at its most extensive under Philip II – of selling municipal office in order to raise cash, both in Spain and in America. It is consequently reasonable to take the view that government in Spain throughout the Habsburg period was typically regional and autonomous, rather than royal or national. Local elites were proud of their regions, and contributed towards a sense of identity for their people, whether in Castile or in Aragon or in Valencia [34]. This did not weaken the crown. On the contrary, it minimised the need for the crown to create a broad and expensive bureaucracy. It also helped to fragment local opposition whenever it arose (e.g. when Saragossa threatened to revolt against Philip II in 1591, not a single other city risked sending military help to the rebels). At one time historians tended to approach the political problems of the monarchy in terms of tension between Castile and other provinces inside or outside the peninsula. Studies of Catalonia, for example, used to present on one side a provincial community enjoying its historic privileges, and on the other, a central state bent on intervening (particularly in the time of Olivares) against those privileges [35]. After the fall of Olivares, it was argued, the non-Castilian realms enjoyed a 'neo-foral' period in which they reverted to virtual self-government. More recently, the greater attention to provincial history has encouraged researchers to study the way provinces ran themselves, rather than look at the provinces primarily through the eyes of Castile. Historians now question whether there was ever a sharp contrast between Castilian intervention and regional autonomy.

14

How, without any modern civil service, was the government able to impose its will when there were disputes? Little could be done except an attempt to maintain a good relationship between crown and regional autonomies, which explains the respect with which the crown treated both the local nobility and the municipal oligarchies. Thompson has described how the pressure of finance and war obliged Philip II to set up central bodies to take care of taxes, recruitment and supplies; but he also shows how in the later years of the reign the crown gave up on centralised control, contracted out for supplies and put more authority into the hands of its regional nobility, who alone could organise local defences [36]. In the great cities, in effect, government was almost wholly autonomous, with tenuous royal control being maintained through the *corregidor* and through the royal courts. Local administration and elites are beginning to receive the attention they deserved [37], and it is now possible to look at the structure of political power from the vantage point of the great cities rather than of the state [38]. This has corrected the traditional perspective that saw only the crown on one side and the people on the other. The urban elites lived in their own universe and made their own rules, so that the power of the crown intruded little into their lives.

In the regions, local elites [39] looked after their own interests without attempting to provoke the central government [40]. A convincing reappraisal of the close links between Castile's government and the regional elites of the monarchy in the later seventeenth century, has emphasised that the constant maintenance of a system of marriages, privileges, distribution of favours and construction of family alliances, had a far greater role in keeping the monarchy together than any government policy could have achieved [41]. It is significant, for example, that when the king of Spain in 1707 abolished definitively the privileges (*fueros*) of the Crown of Aragon, the strongest protests came from within Castile, from the group of nobles whose interests, family links and property holdings tied them closely to the provinces of Aragon.

At the lower level, traditional structures were based on community authority. Many villages and towns continued the medieval practice of self-government based on the *concejo abierto* (village council), but by the sixteenth century much of this was a memory and communal decision-making was more to be found in economic structures, mainly agriculture, than in political life. Community solidarity continued, however, to exist in very many regions that shared common customs, language and domestic economy. Much of the reality of political life in pre-industrial Spain was based at this local level, from which external authority (whether of king or lord or Church) was brusquely excluded, and within which both loyalties and conflicts, often kin-based, were frequently contained [42]. The writer Ortega y Gasset admitted in 1931 that 'the province is the only vital reality that exists in Spain'. In many major cities, authority from generation to generation was jealously divided between groups of families and any attempt to upset the equilibrium provoked violence [43]. A recent study by Helen Nader has put forward the interesting conclusion that the extent of 'liberty' (a medieval concept of self-government) in Castile in fact strengthened the crown by reducing conflict [44].

In conclusion, from the time of Ferdinand and Isabella to the reign of the last Habsburg there was no dramatic advance of state power in Castile or in Spain. This necessarily modifies our view of the extent and efficacy of royal authority. Foreign visitors with only a superficial knowledge of the country claimed to see tyranny and absolutism. Some went so far as to proclaim that Philip II was an 'absolute' ruler. The fact is that monarchy, though in principle 'absolute', remained firmly decentralised throughout the period, and in an association of multiple kingdoms such as peninsular Spain, local autonomy was not necessarily a weakness and could often be a strength.

How did the crown pay its way? The most fundamental cash resource of Spain was the gold and silver it began to receive from the New World in the reign of Charles V (see Chapter 3). The crown did not have sufficient authority to set up absolutism or a national bureaucracy, but in the area of internal finance it made a determined effort to impose its will. Ferdinand and Isabella began the policy of debt [45] and created both personnel and mechanisms (such as *juros*) to deal with it. Under Charles V a more sophisticated system prepared Castile for its long career of imperial finance [46]. The Council of Finance, which evolved from 1523, was responsible for the financing not only of Castile but of all royal enterprises throughout the monarchy, making it unique among the administrative bodies. The alarming increase in government debt has been extensively studied and the impact of fiscality on Castile is well known [47]; taxes rose steadily throughout the sixteenth and early seventeenth centuries, and fell only in the later seventeenth. Though it may seem that by stepping up taxation the state was helping to increase its authority, precisely the reverse happened in Spain, where the crown was obliged to take the highly negative step of giving up areas of its jurisdiction. This occurred in two main ways: real tax income was assigned away to creditors in order to repay long-term debts (*juros*), and important areas of patronage were alienated in order to obtain ready cash. The granting of tax income as *juros* was so extensive that by the end of the sixteenth century the crown had mortgaged virtually all its regular income, and relied heavily on the special grants or *servicios* made by the Cortes. The sale of offices in Castile, known in the fifteenth century and attempted by Charles V in the 1520s, began on a large scale in the 1540s and involved the widespread alienation of municipal posts formerly in crown patronage: between 1543 and 1584 in Castile over 2928 posts of *regidor* (city councillor) were sold [48]. In the early seventeenth century the crown also sold townships (the so-called 'sale of vassals') [49]. It is difficult not to conclude (as Helen Nader does) [44] that the consequence of such alienations not so much a decrease in crown authority as an increase in the political and economic 'liberty' of local communities.

In countries such as England the big obstacle to crown taxation was the claim of parliament to advise and control it. What happened in Spain? One traditional view of the Cortes of Castile during the Habsburg period is that it was 'little more than a rubber stamp', with royal authority supreme in the decadent seventeenth century. That view is no longer tenable. The considerable increase in the grants (*servicios*) voted by the Cortes, which made up about a quarter of royal income in the 1570s but rose to over half in the early seventeenth century, meant that ironically the crown began to depend heavily on them. The Cortes took the opportunity to criticise the long, expensive war in the Netherlands, and to demand a voice in policy in return for granting the *servicios*. In the closing years of Philip II and during the reign of his son, there was an impressive outbreak of constitutionalism in Castile, with members of the Cortes openly proclaiming contractual and democratic principles. Cortes sessions also became more regular, rising to an average of eight months a year as compared to less than two months a year in the mid-sixteenth century [50]. Government ministers bullied and bribed, but from 1600 were forced to accept a contractual agreement that if taxes were voted grievances must be redressed. It is clear that in Castile, as elsewhere in western Europe, there were successful moves to put taxation on a constitutional basis. Though the Cortes of Castile were never summoned during the late seventeenth century (those in the Crown of Aragon were) the government continued to consult directly with the municipalities normally represented there [51]. The constitutional initiative of the Cortes should of course be set in context: it was a short-term achievement, the taxes themselves were usually granted, and no political advantages were gained. But the whole matter is clear testimony to an active political consciousness among the ruling elite of the cities of Castile.

Was there opposition to and popular protest against government? Non-Spanish historians have suggested that Spain of the Golden Age was a society that accepted the rule of 'law' and in which respect for law was shown by a passion for litigation [20]. The view from inside Spain is somewhat different, and it may be argued that the proliferation of lawsuits proves just the opposite, that Spaniards (then as now) [52] ignored the laws. Historians have had to base their conclusions on the somewhat limited evidence of royal courts, where the documentation is accessible but does not tell the whole story. The vital evidence of courts controlled by nobles and the Church has seldom been explored. Among other things, court papers shed light on the way that discontent and resistance might surface in society.

Early modern Spain was no more oppressed by those in power than any other state in Western Europe. The crown always took care to have mechanisms of consultation, even if Cortes were not called, and the writings of the *arbitristas*, who were never slow to air grievances, are evidence of the considerable freedom of public discussion to be found in the country [53]. At the same time the extensive in-fighting among elite groups, both in the provinces and at the king's court, helped to make political alternatives available. There was, for example, considerable conflict between the factions of the duke of Alba and the prince of Eboli at the court of Philip II, and there were serious differences between a war party and a peace party at the court of Philip III. Political intrigue also bred little conspiracies, in which the prophecies of visionaries could play a part [54]. It has been too frequently assumed that in Spain there was no liberty to differ or to speak out, an assumption based no doubt on the existence of an Inquisition. However, no convincing evidence has ever been produced that thought-control existed or could have existed. By contrast there is ample evidence of the preference of Spaniards for freedom (expressed openly in writings which never hesitated to criticise injustice) and especially in a rich tradition of political thought, notably represented by the Jesuit thinkers of the late sixteenth century [55]. The absolutist theories of a writer like Juan Fernández Medrano, who claimed that 'subjects are obliged to obey princes even when these order something against the interests of the people and against civil justice' (1602), may be balanced by theories of more democratic writers. Among the latter one may cite the writings of the Jesuit Juan de Mariana, or the claim of a member of the Cortes in 1621 that 'the king has no absolute power', or the opinion of Diego Pérez de Mesa, who asserted in the same decade that 'all subjects are naturally free and fundamentally equal' [56]. Spanish thinkers were heavily influenced by foreign, especially Italian, theorists, and though some of their writings have an old-fashioned air there were also many who were not only aware of the main issues of their day but also made pioneering and positive contributions to political thinking. There is little reason to treat Spain as a case apart, as though it were a tyranny or an oriental despotism (significantly, the attacks of Mariana and Suárez against tyranny, written around 1600, were condemned in Paris and in London but never in Madrid). In its broad lines of evolution, as Maravall has convincingly shown [17], Spanish thought shared much with the Western tradition. Political theory could be turned into action only with the support of elite groups, something that happened in the period of the Comuneros. In the same way, elite groups who controlled the great cities found their voice in the early 1600s, when the Cortes representative for Granada led the opposition to Olivares [57].

It is sometimes said that in contrast to the rest of Europe, Spain had no popular rebellions. The reverse is true. Spaniards were normal people, ready to rise against oppression, whether state, noble or ecclesiastical. In 1520, the great turmoil of the Comunidades [58] – which included substantial popular agitation [59] – initiated the large-scale movements of the early modern period. Thereafter we know of few major risings until the Granada revolts of the Moriscos in 1569, but in the meantime many dissatisfied Moriscos contributed hugely to public disorder by their participation in banditry in the eastern half of the peninsula [60]. After the Morisco expulsions of 1609–14, however, it was the turn of the Christian population, both in the south and in Valencia, to take on the role of the depressed and exploited; moreover, the crisis conditions of the early century provoked discontent. Among countryside revolts to have been studied are those of 1640 in Catalonia [35], 1648–52 in Andalusia [61], and 1688 and 1693 on the Mediterranean coast [62]. Since they covered an extensive area they usually provoked armed repression. By contrast, force was not normally the method chosen to pacify the many urban agitations that occurred regularly all over Spain, especially in Castile [63]. A great many small revolts were directed not against royal government but against local authorities and noble or Church jurisdictions (as in Valencia in 1693 and again during the War of Succession). They did not affect the state, and documentation on them frequently escapes the attention of the researcher. A form of social protest similar to revolt was banditry, very common during the seventeenth century in the Mediterranean provinces of Spain. The phenomenon has been best studied in Catalonia [64]. Another common type of protest, which took on serious dimensions in an age of constant war, was directed against recruitment for military service. Its impact in Castile has been brilliantly studied by Ruth Mackay [65].

Like other European nations in the mid-seventeenth century, Spain faced a crisis of government that called for higher taxation and logically provoked discontent. The problem of taxation affected not only issues of regional autonomy and central authority within the peninsula, but also provoked tension between Spain and other states of the monarchy. Italians, for example, felt that they were being exploited by Spaniards. Interpretations of the period of crisis, stretching from the events in Aragon in 1591 to the Portuguese and Catalan revolts of 1640, the Naples revolt of 1647–48 and the Palermo rebellion of 1674, are useful yet still require further analysis. Within the peninsula, for example, use of the word 'revolt' can be highly misleading. It is impossible to talk of 'the revolt of Aragon' in 1591 (there was no such revolt, troubles being restricted to Saragossa). The so-called 'revolt of the Catalans' was far more complex than either the notion of 'revolt' or the old image of 'Catalonia vs Castile' might imply. Elliott shows clearly that in 1640 much of the wrath in the principality was in fact directed by ordinary Catalans against their own ruling classes, and few favoured the alliance with France. Sanabre's classic study [66] documents convincingly the opposition of the population to the French. In the post-1653 period, after the recovery of Barcelona, the elites inevitably played down their part in events, but there is growing evidence that the rebels were never more than a small faction. Recently Vidal Pla has looked at the evolution of the royalist party in the province and shows how, while 'the higher nobility abandoned at once the political programme of Pau Claris' and the duchess of Cardona organised pro-royalist resistance from her estates, after 1643 there was widespread defection to the cause of Philip IV. 'The Generalitat, representing the political revolution, and the peasant farmers, representing the popular revolution, had a coincidence of interests in July 1640; but the unity did not last and contradictions between nobles and peasant farmers opened up, leading to popular uprisings throughout the war years' [67].

This picture helps to shift the focus from the old image of a deep-rooted and permanent conflict between Castile on one hand and Catalonia on the other. The reconciliation of the two in the late seventeenth century has been firmly demonstrated [68], making it difficult to accept the simplistic view that Catalonia once again 'revolted' during the War of Succession. Apart from clear evidence that the commercial elite of the two chief ports (Barcelona and Mataró) supported the archduke between 1705 and 1714 with the intention of gaining trade advantages [69], there is little evidence of any widespread rebellion in Catalonia, current research tending to show that most Catalans were neutral and merely supported whichever side happened to be dominant at the time [70]. This brings the picture into line with what we know of the other realms of the Crown of Aragon, where one finds a similar lack of evidence for rebellion. There were notable defections to the Allied cause, but the overwhelming bulk of the elite and of the towns remained solidly faithful to Philip V, declaring for the pretender only when military occupation gave them no other alternative [93].

What changes came with Bourbon power? The administrative changes brought about by the new Bourbon monarchy during the War of

Succession were of capital importance and represent the first major step taken since the epoch of the Catholic Monarchs, towards the creation of a united Spain [71]. The domestic policy of the government was influenced by the events of the war – above all, the rebellion of several provinces and the treason of leading nobles – rather than by any wish to impose absolutist control. Philip V had been brought up to believe in the political theories of his grandfather, Louis XIV, but he had a will of his own and his policies did not always please the French government [72]. Two main changes were brought about by his regime: administration became centred on Madrid after the abolition in 1707 and 1714 of the *fueros* of the Crown of Aragon, and state taxes were centralised and simplified. Customs barriers between the different kingdoms of the peninsula were abolished or reduced. A subsequent attempt in 1717 to unify the Spanish market by abolishing customs barriers between Castile and the Basque provinces, failed because of opposition from the small producers in the north.

The integration of the eastern provinces into a national state gave Spain's government, for the first time in its history, the material resources to pursue the belligerent policies favoured by Philip and his advisers. Three main areas were affected: treasury receipts increased, administrative control was established and a new army and navy were created. For the first time, Spain as a political entity came into existence. All the reforms had their origin in policies that French advisers had implemented during the War of Succession. As a result, Cardinal Alberoni and his successors, with the active encouragement of Philip V, dreamed of restoring Spain's power on the international scene.

3 The Making and Unmaking of Empire

What was the 'Spanish empire'? The imperial idea. How did Spain win its empire? Problems of government and control. How did the empire survive so long? Pressures of war and rebellion in the empire.

'Since God created the world there has been no empire in it as extensive as that of Spain, for from its rising to its setting the sun never ceases to shine for one instant on its lands', was the proud boast in 1655 of the writer Francisco Ugarte de Hermosa. Spanish preponderance was the most obvious reality in European politics during the century 1560–1660, and its decay in subsequent decades no less obvious. Great-power status inevitably created hostile foreign attitudes, which were condemned by a conservative Spanish writer in 1914 as the 'Black Legend' [73]. He maintained that foreigners were bent on denigrating the actions and character of Spaniards, their alleged misdeeds in Europe and America and the supposed cruelty of the Inquisition. Anti-Spanish propaganda was a natural consequence of Spain's great epoch of power under Philip II, and became widespread in Western Europe from the later sixteenth century, stimulated by the Italian wars, the Dutch revolt and the Armada years in England [74]. Curiously, the Spaniards developed no propaganda machine of their own (Spanish printing presses were not as active as those in northern Europe) and their case found no defender. The truth about what happened in the empire (especially with regard to the Inquisition, see Chapter 5) continued to be the subject of polemic and especially among Spaniards.

What was the 'Spanish empire'? By the end of the reign of the Catholic Monarchs, the humanist Nebrija was claiming for his country's possessions 'the title of Empire' [75]. Commentators in subsequent generations were unanimous that Ferdinand the Catholic, through acquisition of territory in Italy and Africa and the New World, 'began the greatness of this immense monarchy' (the writer Fernández de Navarrete, in 1626). Almost from the beginning, then, there was an intentional confusion between the concepts of 'monarchy' and 'empire'. 'Empire' normally suggested, in the manner of the 'Roman empire', conquest and occupation, words which in Spain's case applied correctly only to the African expeditions and the Canary Islands [76]. But some of the realms in the monarchy – Naples, Navarre (and, much later, Portugal) – were also taken over with the help of troops, so that in some sense they could also be described as occupied, even though in each case the crown claimed the territory only through dynastic right and never treated its peoples as conquered. All three realms continued to exist within the monarchy on much the same terms as Aragon. There remained territories of the 'empire' that were invaded without any real concern for their native system of government. They included the African forts and the Canary Islands, as well as various parts of the American continent and the Philippine Islands: all these were effectively treated as 'colonies' that came under the direct rule of the crown of Castile.

The 'imperial idea'. It has been debated whether there was any 'imperial idea' in Spain at this time. Charles V never had a grandiose image of what his territories might signify. He left formulation of 'imperial' theory to his advisers, notably his Chancellor the Piedmontese noble Gattinara, for whom the word 'empire' meant the capacity to exercise sovereign power, without connotations of international expansion [77]. In the early years of his reign there was strong internal opposition, expressed most openly in the Comunidades revolt, to the idea of empire, which it was felt would make the country into a junior partner of foreign interests. 'Empire' was seen as a German, foreign, concept, alien to the real interests of Spain. Many members of the Dominican order continued for a long time to oppose the concept of universal monarchy if it threatened the integrity of their homeland [75; p. 127]. Indeed, persistent anti-imperial sentiments together with the conviction that Spain's future lay in the Mediterranean and not in Europe, can be found in writers throughout the period of the Habsburg dynasty.

Nevertheless, association with the other states forming the 'multiple monarchy' made the idea of 'empire' appear attractive. By the late sixteenth century Pedro Salazar de Mendoza argued that the word 'monarchy' was no longer appropriate, because 'the empire of Spain' is twenty times greater than that of the Romans'; and Juan de Salazar in 1619 turned the argument round to say that 'the empire of Spain is rightly called a monarchy, if by monarchy one means the lordship of almost the whole world'. In the course of time there was a growing number of those who felt that Spain had a destiny to rule [78], and when they said Spain they usually meant 'Castile'. This imperialist attitude, however, was always balanced by the contrary opinion of many who felt that it was not Spain's role to impose itself on others. The two conflicting trends could be found throughout Spain's career as an imperial power, surfacing not only in public learned debate (such as the famous disputation in 1550 between Las Casas and Sepúlveda) but even in closed meetings of the king's council. In a brilliant study of Philip II's secretary Antonio Pérez, Marañón identified the two principal opinions as being on one hand the imperialist attitude of the duke of Alba, and on the other the 'liberal' views of Ruy Gómez, prince of Eboli [25]. It is now agreed that there was no clear distinction of ideas between the Alba and the Eboli groupings. Inevitably, imperialist ideas could always be found among Spaniards. The suggestion has been made that Philip II also had an aggressive 'imperial idea', identifiable as a 'grand strategy' or 'messianic imperialism' [79]. The fact that neither the king nor his principal advisers (Eboli, Cardinal Granvelle, the duke of Alba) ever in their lives uttered a word in favour of aggressive policies of annexation tends to throw doubt on the validity of the argument.

How did Spain win its empire [80] ? Comprehensible pride in Spain's leadership of the monarchy gave rise almost from the beginning to the belief that Spain had single-handedly created it, through its own immense power and wealth. This view passed into the textbooks. Leading historians have presented Spain as 'superior [in banking] to the north of Europe, first in Europe in war technology, the first modern state in Europe' [81], and as enjoying 'massive military capabilities and inexhaustible financial resources' [78; p. 43]. These views have to be set beside the fact that Spain was almost a backwater of the continent, and empire came about exclusively through dynastic succession: in Naples, Navarre and the union in the peninsula itself of Castile and Aragon under Charles V. 'Conquest' certainly played a role, but usually to back up dynastic right. Spanish soldiers undeniably made their mark on Europe, but not because they were part of a programme of military expansion. Their military training, tactics and armaments were reformed during campaigns in Italy around the year 1500, thanks in part to the initiative of their commander Gonzalo Fernández de Córdoba, known as the 'Great Captain'. The reforms, however, were also common to soldiers of other nations involved in the Italian wars, and Spain at no time experienced any 'military revolution' in the troops or resources at its disposal.

In the reign of the emperor Charles V Spain played very little part in international enterprises. Spanish troops took part in Charles's victory at Pavia (1525) and in the capture of Tunis (1535), as well as in the battle of Mühlberg (1547), but none of these campaigns affected Spain or was of benefit to it. Spain, consequently, was not actively at war and had little to win or lose with the emperor's European policies. It follows that the peninsula remained at peace for half a century after the Comunidades of 1520. Not surprisingly, some writers came to lament the long peace and the consequent loss of military expertise. The writer Jéronimo de Urrea in 1566 deplored 'the decline of the martial arts in the Spanish infantry of our time'; and in the Council of War in 1562 the 'peace that has reigned here for so many years' was blamed for the defenceless state of the realm.

Spain's empire was almost unique, because it was not founded on expansion and did not seek further expansion. It held on to three or four forts on the North African coast for security reasons, and for the same reason occupied the port of Finale (1570) on the Mediterranean coast near Genoa. Apart from that, it never embarked on a career of conquest. In the New World so-called 'conquest' was a piecemeal effort carried out by bands of conquistadors and adventurers rather than by any official military action, for with rare exceptions there were no government forces active in the New World until the eighteenth century. Moreover, a bare half-century after the fall of Mexico to Cortés, in 1573 Philip II declared by law that all further conquests in America were to cease. The law also affected the Philippines, where the Spaniards since their arrival in 1565 never controlled more than the small area around the town of Manila.

The reason for this absence of 'conquest' is easy to pinpoint. Castile, which directed the imperial effort, never had sufficient men or resources with which to create or sustain great-power status. Its small population and weak economy (see Chapter 4) ill served the purposes of empire building. Fortunately, however, Castile was the chief partner in the multiple monarchy and could look to its foreign allies for support. It could offer them many benefits that participation in empire building might bring: for the elite, honours; for manufacturers and traders, markets and profits; for the common people, employment in the armed forces. In consequence, Spanish power succeeded in becoming substantial and awesome not because it drew on Castile alone, but because it could attract all its allies into a common venture. The first to benefit from this were the peoples of the Spanish peninsula, who were able to take part in a global enterprise to which their own resources in isolation did not give access. The second to benefit were all the nations in the 'multiple monarchy'. In the 1520s Charles V opened sectors of the New World to Netherlands, German and Portuguese business interests [82]. A decade or so later the government began to exclude non-Spaniards from America, but the exclusion never worked in practice.

In Europe the role of allies was fundamental, above all in the areas of war and of finance. Allies supplied the manpower that gave Spain a military role. Since the time of the Great Captain Gonzalo de Córdoba around 1500, Castilian soldiers serving in Italy were grouped into infantry regiments called '*tercios*' [83], which did not receive a formal organisation until the Ordinance decreed by Charles V in Genoa in 1536. They were only a small solution to the problem created by imperial responsibilities. With its small population of just over five million people, Castile was at no time in a condition to produce enough manpower to service the needs of war and peace overseas. It exported thousands of soldiers [36; pp. 103–7] but was unable to draw on the other realms of the peninsula, whose laws normally restricted their recruits from serving abroad. Like other European governments, Castile therefore had to recruit from its partners in the monarchy and from foreign countries. Throughout the great centuries of empire, Spaniards always remained a minority in the so-called 'Spanish' armies. Spaniards were seldom more than one-tenth of the total of troops that the government helped to maintain in Flanders [84], where the army usually consisted of infantry drawn from the Netherlands, Italy and Germany. In the same way, Castile was unable to supply enough trained officers for the troops. Up to the mid-sixteenth century many Castilian nobles distinguished themselves in the army in Europe, but thereafter Italian and Belgian generals often supplanted them. The elites of the monarchy looked forward to obtaining honour and status for themselves by serving in the armies and imperial administration of the crown. The best-known actions of the 'Spanish' army were the work of non-Spaniards. From the 'Spanish' victory of St Quentin in 1557 (won by a mainly Netherlandish army commanded by the non-Spaniards the duke of Savoy and the earl of Egmont) to the 'Spanish' defeat at Rocroi in 1643 (lost by a mainly Netherlandish-German army commanded by a Portuguese general), the power of Spain was always determined by the contributions that could be made by its allies. Apart from the duke of Alba, the two most outstanding military commanders of the Spanish army were Italians: Alessandro Farnese and Ambrogio Spinola. The international make-up of the 'multiple monarchy' was equally visible at sea. Castilians were not notable seafarers, and under Ferdinand the Catholic naval forces in the Mediterranean tended to be commanded by Catalans and Sicilians. Charles V had few naval forces in the area until the Genoese fleet of Andrea Doria opted to join him in 1528, and thereafter the Italians were always the mainstay of Spanish sea power in southern Europe (at Lepanto in 1571, for example, they supplied two-thirds of the ships and men).

The role of allies in financing the empire was also fundamental. From the moment the Spanish government began to get involved in military and naval enterprises outside the peninsula, it faced the problem of financing them. The resources of the Castilian treasury, deeply in debt from the time of Ferdinand and Isabella, were inadequate. Already from that period, however, the rulers of Spain were making use of the mechanism of 'credit'. In the early sixteenth century there were no public banks, and no generally accepted currency except pure gold or silver. To make payments abroad to financiers, suppliers and its own troops, governments (like traders) had to use credit notes called 'bills of exchange'. There were many Castilian bankers who took part actively in the credit business. But when the shipments of precious metal from America began (see Chapter 4), the Castilians were soon pushed out of the way in the rush to offer credit in exchange for New World bullion. Italian bankers, mainly Genoese, had played an important part in financing the early Spanish voyages to the New World, and now reaped their rewards in Seville, Spain's chief port to the Indies. The Genoese dominated and financed the high tide of Spain's empire. Despite the attempts to weaken their role, from 1557 (with the accession of Philip II) to 1627 they decided the financial destinies of Spain. The foreign financiers, it has been pointed out by the leading authority on the subject, dominated Spain's business affairs for two centuries [85]. Spaniards often objected strongly to their role. 'All the millions that come from our Indies, are taken by foreigners to their cities', Tomás de Mercado wrote in 1571. However, commentators who presented a picture of greedy foreign financiers feeding on the wealth of Spain, failed to understand that Spain needed their help in order to set up a network of international payments for trade and for war.

Backed by substantial support from its allies, Spain could take on its imperial role and the costs of war [86]. Most historians accept the verdict of the Venetian ambassador in 1559 that Philip II aimed 'not to wage war so he can add to his kingdoms, but to wage peace so that he can keep the lands he has'. But 'defensive' policies inevitably became aggressive (the Armada in 1588 and the invasion of France in 1590 are typical examples), for Spain had to protect its interests. The emergence of Spain as a military and naval power occurred principally in the late sixteenth century, as Thompson has demonstrated. The exercise of extensive military power bred a chauvinism among Castilians that other nations, notably Protestant England, felt they should resist. 'We are hated and abhorred', lamented a Spanish writer in 1594, 'and all because of the wars'.

Problems of government and control. From the beginning Spaniards took their imperial enterprise seriously, notably in the New World where they attempted to eliminate what seemed to them evil and attempted to replace it with what was good. The crown was second to none in its concern for its subjects, the Indians and other natives. Queen Isabella forbade enslavement of natives, and both Charles V and Philip II backed Las Casas in his attempts to protect the Indians, notably through the New Laws of 1542. The evidence for their concern may still be consulted in the pages of the law codes they drew up. At every stage the Spaniards attempted to remedy problems through legislation, which some have seen as the most enlightened body of laws ever drawn up till then by an imperial power. The legislation, however, has tended to divide historians into two schools of thought. First are those who take the laws at face value and use them to appraise the functioning of the empire. Second are those who look at the way the empire functioned in practice rather than the way indicated by the laws. At every point the two approaches have led to widely divergent conclusions, often influenced by political ideology.

In the non-Castilian realms the crown's chief liaison officer was the viceroy, a post made necessary first by Ferdinand's absence from his realms of Aragon and later by the clear impossibility of any monarch being able to rule personally in distant realms such as Italy or America. Questions of finance and of law and order inevitably impelled all viceroys to action, thereby bringing royal law into conflict with local privileges. It is clear from the example of Catalonia that viceroys were sometimes able to tamper with the local Cortes, and when acting in conjunction with the king's court of justice, the Audiencia (established in Barcelona in 1493, in Valencia in 1543), the viceroy could issue 'royal' decrees. Though viceroys might win their way over a broad range of issues, they were always aware that the argument must never be forced against local interests [87], and on balance it is doubtful if royal authority throughout the early modern period was ever permanently extended through its viceroys.

Pressures of war and rebellion in the 'empire'. Because most territories in the empire were self-governing and Spain never came to develop an imperial bureaucracy, the main cost incurred was in defence rather than in administration. The demands of war always used up the bulk of government money. The financial implications of war during the 'imperial century', 1560–1660, dragged Castile into foreign commitments that came to absorb the bulk of state revenue. Repayment of state bonds (*juros*) for loans by bankers and others, absorbed by the end of Charles V's reign in 1556 some 68 per cent of normal Castilian revenue. By 1565 the figure was up to 84 per cent, and by the end of Philip's reign in 1598 the total *juro* debt was nearly eight times that of annual revenue. The cost of imperialism was clearly ruinous: in 1634, under Olivares, over

93 per cent of expenditure was earmarked for foreign policy. Felipe Ruiz Martín concludes that 'war cut short the positive evolution of Spain by absorbing resources which would normally have served to increase production. ... The proliferation of *juros* checked growth. ... War, for Spain, had a decisive influence on the economic process' [86].

But the costs were not borne only by Spain, nor was the impact of war limited to Spain alone [88]. A good example is the battle of Lepanto (1571), the famous naval victory of Christians over Turks. Parker and Thompson have shown clearly that tax grants made by the papacy to Spain covered the greater part of Spain's costs [89]. In the same way, at every stage of imperial history it was the Italian, German and other foreign bankers who supplied the credit that made it possible to launch military campaigns.

Though much research exists on finances, relatively little has been done on the mechanics of Spanish imperialism or on the part Spanish resources played in relation to those of other countries. There is no adequate history of the Spanish military forces in the age of empire, though an excellent general survey has been done by Jan Glete [90]. Aspects of science and technology are touched on by Goodman [91]. On questions of manpower, Parker has convincingly studied the military relationship between the peninsula and the Netherlands, and in the process has given us splendid insight into the mechanics of the sixteenth-century army in Flanders [84], [92]. Thompson has also looked at recruitment during the same period, but for the entire seventeenth century we remain in the dark about the recruitment, officering and administration of the Spanish forces. We only know that by the War of Succession the army was no match for its enemies, relied heavily on foreigners as general officers, and won victories only when aided by the French army [93]. Thanks to the extensive research generated by commemoration of the 1588 Armada in 1988, there are now many good studies of naval affairs [94]. Spain's capability in shipbuilding is not in doubt: well into the late seventeenth century, the epoch of alleged decline, a sample of 239 vessels used in the American trade shows that only 37 per cent were foreign-built, the rest being constructed either in America or in Spain, mainly in Basque shipyards. On the supply of war-materials, there is a key study of the iron industry of northern Spain [95], but little information about armaments, gunpowder, and related items has yet emerged, leaving one to suspect that Spain had little. This is not wholly surprising, since Spain's wars tended to be fought abroad, not at home, and it was more sensible to supply the army of Flanders from the more industrialised Netherlands and Liège, and the army of Milan from Milan itself. The peninsula, so easily invaded during the War of Succession, was just as defenceless over a century earlier, when the English in 1596 captured and held Cadiz for three weeks. The evidence suggests not so much a decline as a failure right from the start, to build up the defences of the peninsula.

The role of Milan and Naples has only recently been given attention by historians [96]. Since Renaissance times, Italy had been the key to European power and hence the theatre of some of Charles V's most important campaigns. By granting Milan to his son Philip in 1540, the Emperor made sure that the Spanish monarchy would hold a strategic prize that thereafter became essential to its survival, for three main reasons: it dominated northern Italy and therefore restricted Venetian, papal and French pretensions; it supplied two key routes to northern Europe, through the 'Spanish road' and through the Valtelline; and it drew on important Italian manpower, armament and banking resources, as well as the naval resources of Genoa. Spain's domination of northern Italy remained at all times the highest priority of Spanish imperial policy, and inevitably invited French intervention in the early seventeenth century, when Olivares made the mistake of pressing Spanish interests to the point of war (1628) over the Mantuan succession.

The relative neglect, until very recently, of diplomatic history has meant that we still do not know enough about the formation of policy and about public opinion, and most of our assumptions about Spanish foreign policy have remained unchanged over the past century. A masterly new multi-volume survey by Ochoa, however, offers important perspectives and information [97]. The pioneering study by Mattingly on diplomacy under Ferdinand the Catholic retains its value [98]. For the early Habsburg period, none of the great career diplomats of the imperial age has been examined in depth, with the notable exception of Bernardino de Mendoza [99]. Of political personalities in the late sixteenth century only Cardinal Granvelle has received detailed attention [100], though many aspects of his fertile career remain to be studied. The important links of the Spanish government with the German Habsburgs have long been neglected, but are now receiving detailed attention [101]. Crucial aspects of policy in the seventeenth century have now been explored in respect of the Twelve Years Truce with the Dutch rebels [102], and the foreign policy objectives of Olivares [103]. Diplomacy, of course, was not a science limited to a single class of officials, and the development of policy has also to be investigated through the work of very many persons, notably military men and ecclesiastics. A case in point is the outstanding role of the Belgian artist, Rubens, as ambassador for Spanish interests in the early seventeenth century. Belgians and Italians played an important role in the diplomatic service of Spain. The professional diplomats of this period were sophisticated and cultured men who did not necessarily give blind obedience to their employers.

From these studies it appears that Spain, while not actively expansionist, was drawn into conflicts by the obvious need to protect its interests, so that it would be unjust to consider its policies as uniformly aggressive. By the same token, priorities were never exclusively ideological, and Spain seldom acted as the secular arm of the Counter Reformation. Despite having good relations with the papacy after the 1550s and a broad agreement on religious aims, Philip II never succeeded in making his political objectives coincide with those of the pope. And yet there was an indubitable chauvinism about Spain's role, with its insistence on preserving honour and *reputación*, that infuriated other Europeans. This negative image abroad, cultivated even by allies of the crown such as Italians and Belgians, helped to perpetuate the Black Legend well into the epoch of the Thirty Years War, and does scant justice to the real differences of opinion that always existed among Spaniards. State documents leave no doubt that there were often quite fundamental disagreements among the policy-makers, though there is little evidence to justify, for example, the old and simplistic picture of two rival policy factions under Philip II, one of the duke of Alba which favoured a 'ruthless' solution to imperial affairs and the other of the prince of Eboli which favoured 'negotiation'. In practice, issues were never seen in such stark 'war' and 'peace' terms. Alba, like any professional soldier, wanted a quick, clean military solution; he thought that this was possible in Flanders just as he later thought it was not possible in England and so opposed the 'war' policy of Granvelle and those who counselled an invasion [104].

A generation of war under Philip II was enough to excite strong reaction, and the subsequent government was in tune with public opinion when it sought peace. The Netherlands revolt was Spain's Vietnam, sucking the money and lives of the interventionists, and like Vietnam it provoked a passionate nation-wide debate: 'no one knows', wrote the Jesuit Juan de Mariana in 1609, 'when this war will end, our losses have been great and the humiliation greater'. Maravall has made a short study of the controversy and has identified it in some measure as opposition to the government [105]. The war, however, culminating as it did with the independence of the Dutch in 1648, had other profound and long-term reverberations: it brought to some a disenchantment with the dream of empire, and sparked off the literature of disillusion produced by *arbitristas* within Castile. As early as 1598 Alamos de Barrientos claimed to see 'our realms defenceless, infested, invaded; the Mediterranean and Atlantic lorded over by the enemy; the Spanish nation worn out, prostrate, discontented and disfavoured; *reputación* and honour laid low'. Such exaggerations were to become the stock-in-trade of subsequent commentators. A generation later, in 1624, an official of the Council of the Indies asked the question, 'Why should we pursue a ruinous war that has gone on for sixty-six years, and is leading us to destruction?' The need to disengage from the whole of the Netherlands without prejudicing imperial security came to be a constant objective of the policy-makers, particularly after 1648.

Though the peace party was influential in Madrid at the turn of the century and under Lerma [106], Spain's professional diplomats – Osuna in Naples and Oñate in Vienna, for example – sounded alarm signals at the continuing threat to Spanish interests from the Dutch, whose fleets had used the Twelve Years Truce to make massive incursions into Portuguese and Spanish territory overseas, and whose agents were active throughout Protestant Europe as well as in Venice and in Bohemia. The drift into conflict with the expiry of the Truce in 1621 formed part of the general European conflagration known as the Thirty Years War [107]. What has become clearer with recent research is that the entire first phase of the war, up to about 1630, and including within it major events such as the occupation of the Palatinate, the Mantuan venture, and the plan for a Baltic fleet [108], was centred round the epic struggle between the United Provinces and Spain [109], a struggle which saw Spain's forces committed on every European front and which terminated in dismal and unquestionable failure, leading Olivares to grieve that 'neither in Flanders nor in Italy have we done anything except lose *reputación*'. The opening of hostilities with France in 1635 was not at first traumatic, since France had little military experience and would soon be preoccupied with its domestic troubles in the Fronde; but the strains imposed on the creaking *monarquía* by war, economic crisis, and French-inspired conspiracies among the elites of Catalonia, Portugal and Naples, brought the whole structure to its knees.

Most surveys of foreign policy terminate with the Peace of Westphalia in 1648 and that of the Pyrenees in 1659. It has been argued with reason that the war effort of these decades cannot be written off simply by citing the defeat at Rocroi (1643), and that in 1652 there was an impressive display of strength with the recapture, on three distinct fronts, of Barcelona, Dunkirk and Casale [110]. Though the truly great territorial losses were still to come, there can be little argument that in the forty years after 1660 Spain lost any real capacity to maintain its international position and was truly 'in decline': the 'imperial century' simply ran out of steam. During the period 1660–1700, which has been imperfectly studied and merits more research, many Spanish statesmen reverted to the traditional Mediterranean-based policies that had predated the great age of empire. Some evidence of this is given in the proposal, first made by Mazarin and then warmly supported in Spain, for the surrender to France of the southern Netherlands in exchange for the provinces of Catalonia lost in 1659. The most astonishing feature of the post-1648 period, however, was the diplomatic revolution by which Spain entered into a close alliance with the Dutch, who were needed for the primary purpose of defending the southern Netherlands and restraining the aggression of Louis XIV [80; p. 412] [111]. The rapprochement attained its apogee in the 1670s with the admission of Dutch garrisons into Spanish fortresses in Flanders and the joint manoeuvres of the Dutch and Spanish fleets in the Mediterranean, culminating in the Protestant admiral De Ruyter giving his life in battle in 1676 for the defence of Catholic Spain.

How did the empire survive so long? The Spanish Empire is considered to have come to an end in 1898, when the United States seized its last territories, Cuba, Puerto Rico and the Philippines. Patriotic feeling among many Spaniards therefore maintains that the empire endured for four centuries, a tribute to its great power. Did it really survive that long? It is a question of definitions and perspective. In the Philippines, for example, the Spaniards never controlled more than a small corner of one of its 7000 islands. In mainland South America, the Spanish hold was no less precarious. There was a continuous Spanish presence, but rarely backed up by 'power'. It is doubtful whether the description of 'empire' had any real meaning in the overseas territories, and the notion of the 'survival' of imperial control is consequently devoid of meaning if there was little control to begin with. In economic terms, as early as the seventeenth century the bulk of the economy of the New World was already in the control of non-Spaniards. By the end of that century most territories in the Caribbean were occupied by other Europeans. When the Americans took over Cuba, they already controlled 85 per cent of its foreign trade. What survived for four centuries was little more than an illusion of empire; the real empire had vanished long before. If the illusion survived, it was because European states made an effort to preserve it, in the way that vultures might wish to prolong the existence of a delectable victim.

Pressures of war and rebellion in the empire. We have seen that Spain's imperial role was made possible only by the joint resources of several countries. It followed ineluctably that those countries soon resented the burden imposed on them, and saw the Spanish connection as a yoke to be thrown off. Already under Charles V there were complaints of the rising cost of the wars in Germany and the Mediterranean: in the Netherlands special taxation rose steeply between the 1530s and the 1560s [112]. The Low Countries, however, were of great strategic and economic value to Spain, whose government felt it should take a hard line when presented with protests. Rebels in the Netherlands presented their cause as a fight for liberty and true religion [113], and Spaniards too came round to emphasising the religious factor. The result was a rapid slide into a war of repression that devoured Spanish military resources for three-quarters of a century [114]. Although the southern Netherlands (Belgium) remained allied to Spain (1579–1713), there too the same protests continued to be made [115]. In Italy the accumulated burden of heavy taxation and Spanish control provoked important rebellions in Naples (1647) [116] and in Messina (1674) [117]. These, considered together with the peninsular rebellions of 1640, demonstrate that the monarchy was breaking apart because of unequal burdens imposed by the imperial programme of Castile.

It was the feeling of dissatisfaction that eventually persuaded the United Provinces, Belgium, Naples and other realms, to sever their link with Spain. Similar motives had impelled the Catalans [35] [66] and Portuguese in 1640 (to say nothing of the abortive plots in Andalusia and in Aragon). However, some Castilians, like Fernández de Navarrete and Olivares, saw the problem in quite a different light: to them it appeared that the weakness of the monarchy derived precisely from the excessive autonomy of each constituent realm, and that Castile alone had been shouldering the burden of empire for the preceding two generations. Each side of the argument was in some measure correct. Naples, the Netherlands, and Portugal were fully sovereign states, with their own separate parliaments, institutions, and laws: all they shared in common was their king, and it was repugnant to them that their interests should always be subordinated to those of Castile. Olivares, for his part, felt that this loose federation of states should be turned into a real fusion of resources. It was not a crazy dream: his contemporary, the Italian priest Campanella, who spent twenty years in a Spanish prison in Naples, also felt that a truly powerful empire could be based on Spain, with all nationalities serving equally in it, Portuguese for example in Castile and Castilians in Portugal. However, in addition to the constant particularism of each state, there were other reasons that by the early seventeenth century helped to undermine Spanish power.

The fundamental fact is that Castile's inadequate manpower and industrial resources (see Chapter 4) made it ill-equipped to sustain an imperial programme for long; in this it had an exact parallel in seventeenth-century Sweden. At most, the country might manage to finance a programme that was being serviced by its allies, which is what in effect happened under Philip II, with Castile paying the bills but its allies supplying the men and the munitions. Catastrophic state debt, however, made it impossible to go on. The obligations of imperial power, moreover, forced Spain to over-extend its commitments: during the Thirty Years War it had fighting units in Bohemia, Germany, Belgium and Italy, with naval forces in Brazil and America and defensive units in north Africa, Portugal and Spain (Philip IV in a burst of misinformed optimism in 1625 declared that he had some 800 000 men under arms throughout the war theatres, and this was before the outbreak of hostilities with France). Finally, the persistent pressure of enemy powers, principally the Dutch up to 1648 and the French after the declaration of war in 1635, put intolerable strains on the overburdened Spanish military machine. In the opening years of the seventeenth century, Spanish ministers recognised the seriousness of the strength arrayed against them: 'we cannot by force of arms reduce those provinces', commented Baltasar de Zúñiga in 1619, referring to the Dutch; by 1635, despite the optimism of Olivares, many approached the conflict against France with dismay. In the circumstances, it may be said that the rise of imperial power from the 1560s was what directly precipitated decline: rise and decay were alternate faces of the same phenomenon, and there was nothing mysterious about the collapse of Spanish hegemony in Europe by about 1660, when the century of preponderance turned full circle.

The collapse of Spanish power in the western world has been surveyed by Hussey [118] and, within the context of Italy, by Alcalá-Zamora [119]. When the War of Succession came in 1702, the government's inability to fight a war on home soil was demonstrated clearly by its heavy reliance on foreign, mainly French troops, and by its almost total reliance on France for basic supplies (armaments, uniforms) [93]. This time there was a determination to be rid of the Habsburg inheritance, and the Spanish Netherlands were placed firmly in the hands of France. The poverty of Spain's war potential, however, was apparently no graver in 1705 than in 1605, so that the idea of a 'decline' is unhelpful: the likely situation was that between these dates Spain had taken only limited steps to enhance its service industries (munitions, gunpowder etc.), and was happy to draw on the resources of its allies in the monarchy. Moreover, while other nations (particularly the France of Louvois) were modernising and nationalising their armies, Spain continued to rely on classic and well-tried methods that had helped its crack regiments, the *tercios*, dominate the battlefields of the early seventeenth century, but proved unsuitable in the conditions of the late century, when the enemy was using new weapons and new techniques. Most surprising of all for a country which relied so heavily on communications, the Spain that had been able to muster enormous armadas in cases of emergency never succeeded in establishing a good regular navy, and throughout the seventeenth century the clearest index to the crumbling of its hegemony is the series of naval defeats it suffered at the hands of the Dutch (from the plate fleet in 1628 to the Downs in 1639), the English (from Drake's sacking of Santo Domingo in 1585 to Blake's attack on the plate fleet in 1657), and the French (from Guetaria in 1638 to the bombardment of Barcelona and Alicante in 1691).

4 Did Spain Decline?

The debate over 'rise' and 'decline'. What 'declined', Spain or its empire?
The crucial role of precious metals. Population change in early modern
times. The agrarian economy. Cultural minorities and the impact of expul-
sions. The influence of international trade. The economic recovery of the
seventeenth century.

The debate over 'rise' and 'decline'. Few ideas have been so deeply
rooted as that of the 'decline of Spain'. It was elaborated first of all
by conservative Spaniards of the Romantic school in the mid-
nineteenth century who looked for an explanation as to why their
country, once the world's greatest power, had come to lose that
greatness [120]. The troubles of the present encouraged them to
idealise a faraway peak of achievement that preceded current failures. In order to make the idea plausible, it was essential to identify in the past an epoch of success (a 'Golden Age'). Since the
concept was above all a moral one it never came to acquire any pre-
cision, and writers threw in a broad range of ingredients in order
to sustain it. This ideologically conservative myth soon gained
acceptance. In the English-speaking world, Hamilton presented
the clearest outline of the 'decline' argument in 1936 [121].
Subsequently in 1961 Elliott reiterated the conservative argument
but modified it in part, stating that 'we are faced with the problem
not so much of the decline of Spain as of the decline of Castile'.
He concluded that 'there are always the same cards, however we
shuffle them' [122]. In various later studies, he developed his
support for the theme of a 'decline of Spain' [123].
    Normally the terms of debate have concentrated on three areas:
Spain's empire, its economy, and its culture. The problem is that
contradictions arise when trying to identify the chronology and

characteristics of success and failure in each of these areas. For example, one scholar sees the Spain of Philip II as 'unquestionably the most powerful state in western Europe', whose 'revenues, dominions and armies were the largest of any European' power, [114; p. 19] while another (W. H. Prescott) saw in it little more than 'the hectic brilliancy of decay'. Inevitably, one possible conclusion [124] is that the data used to sustain the idea of a decline are so contradictory that the concept should be discarded as meaningless. That leaves, certainly, one crucial question: what happened in Spain's case for historians to be dedicating more time to its failures than to its successes? James Casey took the analysis one step further by suggesting that the economy of Spain had really failed to develop and could be seen as a case of 'failed transition' [125]. James Thomson, who also looked principally at economic issues, presented a carefully balanced survey of some of the problems involved in the controversy [126]. He agreed about the difficulty of analysing 'decline', commented that the various arguments of historians reflected 'different aspects of an extremely complex reality', and opted for an explanation of Spain's perennial weakness along the lines of the country's 'dependence' on outside factors.

There is little disagreement on the basic facts: Spain certainly had a period of remarkable success. Before the age of empire, the Iberian peninsula had a poor economy and few resources; even food had to be imported. In the first half of the sixteenth century, suddenly, Castile experienced a phase of unprecedented prosperity: industry expanded, population increased, output rose. This development was logical: prosperity was in part self-generated, for the rest of Western Europe was in a phase of expansion during the same period. However, there were also fundamental exterior factors. Castile now formed part of a worldwide empire and as a result benefited from it in many ways. The riches, success and power that accrued to Castile came from the resources of the communities in the multiple monarchy, not only from Castile itself. Spanish literature acquired the advantage, available to no other nation, of being able to publish Spanish books in several other states that formed part of the empire. The most important of the outside benefits gained by Spaniards was the import of the treasures of the New World.

The crucial role of precious metals. One factor stands out as contributing to economic growth in Castile and Spain's emergence as a European power: the import of precious metals from America. Without the injection of wealth that stimulated demand, gave life to commerce, and enriched sections of the population, no expansion would have been possible. The wealth also helped to pay for the military costs of the monarchy. All attention turned to Spain and its fabulous American mines. Between 1540 and 1700 the New World produced around fifty thousand tons of silver, a quantity that doubled the existing stock of silver in Europe, with profound consequences for its economy. Over seventy per cent of this production came from the famous site at Potosí. There are no reliable figures for the amounts of metal transported across the Atlantic, but the official imports registered at Seville indicate that between 1500 and 1650 over a hundred and eighty tons of gold and sixteen thousand tons of silver were sent from the New World to Spain.

The import of bullion into Spain accelerated the 'price revolution' and was seen by Hamilton [127] as its principal cause, though historians now agree that the so-called 'revolution' was common to all European countries and was also set in motion by population increase and agrarian change. In order to finance trade and pay for military costs, Spaniards also had to export bullion. Since those who really controlled the trade system were foreign bankers, it was to them that the bullion and profits went rather than to Spain [128]. A consequence was that throughout the great age of trade the peninsula functioned less as exporter or importer than merely as a channel for the distribution to other countries of wealth received from the colonies. With good reason did the merchants of Seville protest (in 1626) that 'our people are without sustenance and income, the foreigners are rich; and Spain, instead of being as a mother to her sons has ended up as a foster-mother, enriching outsiders and neglecting her own'. After the midseventeenth century the value of bullion began to fall: it became superfluous to the European trade process and vast quantities were re-exported to Asia [129]. The situation made it possible for Castile in the late century (by the decrees of 1680 and 1686) to stabilise its currency without calling on further resources [130].

Population change in early modern times. In general, Spain coincides with European trends of growth in the sixteenth century and deceleration in the early seventeenth. There can be little dispute over the main pattern observable in most of the peninsula [131]: a slow increase from the late fifteenth into the early sixteenth century, with a marked and sometimes dramatic expansion in the central decades of the century to 1590, then a steep fall from approximately 1590 to 1650, and a slow recovery from 1660 into the early eighteenth century. Expansion in the first half of the sixteenth century was helped by the absence of any major epidemics, and by the lack of foreign wars. The mid-century years show considerable evidence of economic growth, with industrial and agricultural expansion, a boom in trade and finance, and urban construction. The expansion can be identified concretely in Old Castile with the commercial boom in towns such as Segovia and Valladolid [132], and in Seville with the expansion of American trade [133]. There was a 78 per cent increase in the population of New Castile between 1528 and 1591, the steepest increase coming after 1560; in Jaén, further south, the increase was also high, at 75.5 per cent. In the final third of the century, however, negative signs increased: there were epidemics, grain shortages and the beginning of direct involvement in military action against the Turks and the Dutch. The symptoms of recession were various, and could be identified all over Europe, but they were clearly visible in many key sectors of the Spanish economy. It is possible too that emigration to America had an adverse effect, though the numbers involved appear not to have been of crisis proportions. From the 1580s, parish records show a definite downswing in birth figures. In most of Spain, the demographic crisis appears to have lasted for two generations, with further desolation wreaked by the great epidemics of 1596–1602 and 1647–54 [134]. The population levels fell so sharply that they were not regained until the middle years of the eighteenth century. Contemporaries continued for generations to make wildly exaggerated claims about the crisis, statistical accuracy not being one of the virtues of the age. There was much introspective pessimism [123], particularly when writers saw stagnation within and military defeat abroad; it is this epoch that many contemporaries and some historians have looked upon as the apogee of 'decline'.

There were variations within this general picture. The demographic experts distinguish between a pattern for 'interior' or peninsular Spain, and another for the periphery or coastal Spain, with recovery occurring earlier in the latter areas. On the Mediterranean coast, in Catalonia, population rose in the early sixteenth century by only 20 per cent, but the rate accelerated to about 75 per cent between the 1550s and the 1620s, in which increase a major role has been attributed to the factor of French immigration (in the parish of Sant Just in Barcelona in 1576–1625 some 23 per cent of men getting married were French) [135]. Thereafter no major interruption appears to have occurred until the crisis of the 1640 rebellion and the serious epidemic of 1654. There was also a significant variant in the north-west, particularly Galicia and Asturias, where the expansion of the sixteenth century was muted, but by contrast the seventeenth in its entirety was one of marked expansion, and only from the 1690s into the eighteenth century was there a sharp demographic reverse [136]. We should also bear in mind that, in Valencia at least, growth rates for Moriscos (one-third of the population) were higher than those for Christians. Thus the great complexity of demographic development in the peninsula makes it difficult to posit one single pattern. In rounded terms, the population of Spain (including the Balearic Islands but excluding the Canaries and Portugal) probably rose from about 5.25 million in the 1480s to a ceiling of about 8 million in the late sixteenth century, remaining after the depression period at around 7 million until the later decades of the eighteenth century.

There are relatively few studies of family structure, the most relevant being those done by David Reher [137]. Specific censuses, such as those made in Castile in 1561 [138] and 1591 [244], have enabled us to understand something of the make-up of population in terms of wealth and profession. Work on the parish records has given further insight into family structure in the peninsula. The mean age of first marriage for women (a crucial determinant of fertility) has been shown to be about 20 years in the Algarve, Valladolid, Cuenca and Mallorca around the mid-sixteenth century. In the mid-seventeenth in the Catalan lands (Girona, Barcelona) and in parts of Valencia (Guadalest, Alicante) there are cases of the age rising to 22, but against this we must balance the various Morisco communities of the period (Extremadura, Valencia) where the mean age varied from 20 down to 18 years [139]. The notably low age of female marriage, in contrast to the standard west European pattern where the mean age of female first marriage was 24 years, has led Casey to suggest that the Spanish demographic pattern was basically non-European [140]. However, it is also certain that in an important part of the peninsula, specifically the north-west including Galicia and northern Portugal, female first marriage in the seventeenth and early eighteenth centuries occurred at about 27 years, bringing this area more into line with western Europe. It has been suggested that the northwest had a 'developed' or modern pattern, and that the centre and south of Spain had an 'archaic' or mediaeval model which was evolving towards the west European model. The significance of these peninsular patterns, which in any case need to be set within a broader context (low age of marriage can also be found in Italy at this period), remains unclear as long as we continue to have little information about other variables. It seems, for example, that the capacity of the low marriage age in Spain to replace population lost by epidemics must have been restricted by the high level of abstinence from marriage, an abstinence dictated either by choice (religion) or economic status (servant girls) or early widowhood (this would affect the frequency of second marriages). Molinié-Bertrand states that in the 1590s 'single women, either widows or celibate, constituted between 20 per cent and 30 per cent of the population of Castilian cities' [244]. The profile suggested by this author on the basis of the 1591 census is that the Castilian woman married at about 18 years, had her first child after about a year, and bore her last child at the age of 35. If this can be confirmed, it offers a period of fertility – some seventeen years – not very different from the 15 years common in the west European pattern. However, the high level of celibacy (notably higher than the 20 per cent maximum posited by Hajnal for western Europe), and the high rate of infant mortality, resulted in inadequate population replacement and therefore in a negative demographic tendency, whose duration still needs to be squared with other population data.

Among the major factors that depleted population were epidemics, emigration and war. Because epidemics prior to the seventeenth century are often poorly documented, it is difficult either to date them or measure their intensity. Detailed work has been done for Castile on outbreaks of the early modern period [134], and on those of the late sixteenth century [141], with surveys of those of 1647–54 [236] and of 1676–85 [252]. There can be no doubt that the epidemics intensified mortality greatly; over one million people died in the seventeenth-century epidemics alone, with death rates sometimes at ten times the normal. In broader perspective, we must note that a mortality crisis of possibly even worse proportions was occurring in Italy at the same period, so the misfortunes of Spain should be seen not in isolation but as part of a general demographic collapse in the Mediterranean.

The overall picture is of a population that was constantly moving and changing. This even affected the interior of Spain, where people moved around with greater frequency than historians once thought. Younger persons tended to move around either to find marriage partners or to find work. Seasonal employment accounted for very large numbers of migrants, of whom many might stay to become part of the resident workforce. A village in Extremadura reported in 1575 that 'most of the people are poor, and they go to Andalusia to earn enough to eat and are gone most of the year' [142]. The best known example of Spanish seasonal emigration is that of the peasants of Galicia, who because of their inadequate landholdings emigrated regularly to Castile and Andalusia to find supplementary work, returning usually to help with their own harvest. In the same way, thousands of French rural labourers crossed the Pyrenees each summer to help gather the Spanish harvest.

Voluntary and involuntary emigration overseas probably had a negative impact. The flow of registered as well as illegal emigrants to the New World may have totalled 250 000 for the whole sixteenth century, and substantially less for the seventeenth, but the official figures merit little confidence and historians have had to resort to estimates [143]. The two great cultural expulsions of the period – that of the Jews in 1492 and that of the Moriscos in 1609–14 – differed in their impact on the peninsula (see Chapter 5). In the case of the expelled Jews, numbers were small and the emigrants of modest economic means, so that the social and economic consequences for the country were minimal. The Morisco expulsions, on the other hand, were significant. The 300 000 Spaniards driven from their homeland represented one-third of the population of Valencia and one-fifth that of Aragon, and the short-term consequences were serious in some areas. But the Moriscos themselves had been declining both in population and in their economic contribution to their landlords [144], so that the overall impact on the Christian economy was not uniformly disastrous, and many nobles were able to accept the expulsions without regret.

Since Spain tended to fight its wars abroad rather than at home, the emigration of soldiers probably affected population adversely.

Because the so-called 'Spanish' army was made up primarily of non-Spaniards, numbers involved were not large. However, the burden fell mainly on Castile, since by their constitutions the non-Castilian realms sent few men abroad. Under Philip II about 9000 men a year were recruited from Spain; in crisis years the totals could double. One may speculate that the absence of many young men from their homes from the 1570s onwards contributed to the fall in the domestic birth rate: this appears to have been the result for example in Cáceres [145]. There were also two important internal wars in the peninsula that affected economy and population: these were the war against Portugal (1640–68), which had profound consequences on Extremadura, and the War of Succession. Even at the time, commentators were aware that Spanish imperialism was exacting a heavy price of Castile's limited population.

The agrarian economy. The economy of pre-industrial Europe was overwhelmingly agricultural, and a basic guide to economic progress in Spain would be the measurement of agrarian productivity. The most common method of doing this has been to use tithe returns as a basis. Since tithes were normally a tenth of produce, the data would allow an accurate estimate of the full harvest to be made. From the many useful studies that have been made [132], [149], it can be seen that the curve for production generally coincides with the curve for population. In the archbishopric of Toledo, a territory that included most of New Castile, cereal production rose steadily from 1460 to 1560, reaching its zenith in the period 1560–80; thereafter, there was a decline until the decade 1640–50, followed by stagnation or by a slow recovery into the late seventeenth century [146]. This general outline could also be found in other areas such as Catalonia and the Basque country, but with significant differences for the seventeenth century. In Catalonia, for example, there was a crisis of agrarian production and therefore a decline in the taxes that nobles received from their estates between the 1620s into the 1660s, a problem further aggravated by the civil conflicts. In general terms, the sixteenth century was one of expanding output and the early seventeenth one of crisis. Once again, we must note the major exception of the north-west of Spain, where the introduction of maize helped to stabilise cereal output and keep population levels high. In Asturias already by 1617 maize was 'the sustenance of the poor people', thus preceding by over a decade its adoption in Galicia [147], and production of the crop remained high throughout the seventeenth century, thereby helping to rescue the northwest from the economic crisis of the rest of the peninsula.

Given the great variety of climate and land use in the peninsula it is obvious that there were significant differences everywhere. We must first of all ask: was there really an increase in production in the sixteenth century? There can be little doubt that no qualitative innovations in technique occurred, and Spanish literature on the topic was – apart from Gabriel Alonso de Herrera's best seller *Agricultura General* (1513) – sparse. Yield ratios, that is, the proportion of grain reaped to grain sown, remained among the lowest in western Europe, in Old Castile at about 4 : 1 in wheat, though higher rates can be found elsewhere. Thus if there was higher output it came about exclusively because more land was put under the plough: towns encroached on their common lands, individuals usurped or bought (from a penurious crown) public royal lands (*baldíos*) [148], cities disputed with the Mesta over rights to pasture. None of this was enough to feed the growing population satisfactorily, but thanks to regular imports, particularly from Sicily, Spain seems to have had no food riots before the early seventeenth century. Second, did the undoubted fall in production in the subsequent period (in Segovia wheat output fell by 30 per cent between the 1580s and 1640 [132]) represent a real decline in food supplies? The answer is almost certainly 'no': output seems to have been adjusted to fit demand from a smaller population. In the village of Torrejoncillo wheat output between 1630 and 1684 fell by over 50 per cent, but the supply per household remained constant since the population had also shrunk. Gonzalo Anes has argued with good reason that the depression probably had positive aspects which helped to overcome the crisis: 'where population decline meant a shrinkage of arable, more pasture became available to feed more livestock. With cultivation reduced to only the best lands, a rise in output per unit sown was an inevitable consequence. The decrease in population guaranteed a proportionally higher return for each worker, and in these areas agricultural surpluses became possible' [149]. Third, there were important changes in the types of crop sown. The most remarkable case is the northwest, where the introduction of maize from the 1630s revolutionised living standards, and in Galicia by the late century represented over three-fourths of all cereals. With a higher yield ratio of up to 50 : 1, and a shorter vegetative cycle that left the land free for other use, maize became the salvation of the poor peasantry. In other parts of Spain, too, changes occurred. The expulsion of the Moriscos, who were for the most part not wheat-eating, allowed land to come back into wheat production for the Christian population. In some areas the higher yield ratio of non-wheat cereals encouraged farmers to shift their crop emphasis (mainly to barley) so as to get more grain, which in any case was desired for feeding livestock: in parts of Andalusia the increase in barley output in the late seventeenth century was four times greater than in wheat. Finally, we know that the availability of land, as wheat production shrank, encouraged a move to *viticulture*; it was a fair commercial decision, but strongly denounced by those who, like the official Caxa de Leruela (1631), felt that wheat (for human mouths) should have priority.

The crucial importance of agriculture has attracted the attention of historians in recent years. Jesús García Fernández has done some pioneering work on systems of cultivation [150]. Vassberg has returned to the debate, popularised by a past generation of scholars such as Joaquín Costa, over the importance of communal exploitation of holdings [151]; he has also contributed usefully to the very complex discussion over the problems of the Castilian economy. Although we now have some fine surveys of the evolution of the rural economy, especially in its ascendant phase [152], there are differing views about why problems arose. Vassberg sums up many opinions when he says that 'the real problem was not meteorological but human: poverty was the result of man-made institutions that were inefficient, and that did not permit the proper utilization of resources'. Among the reasons offered by historians for this situation are: inequitable land distribution, the preference of the communal system for antiquated techniques of exploitation (such as rotation methods and use of mules), the difficulty of obtaining cash or credit for investment in the soil (hence the increase in rural debt, provoked by the use of the *censo*), and the burden of rents and taxes. Discussion on all these points is necessarily open-ended, since there were immense variations throughout the peninsula. The situation of the peasant could change substantially, for example, depending on whose jurisdiction he fell under [153]. In some parts of Aragon and in post-Morisco Valencia the dependence of peasants on the lords was heavy; but even in free Castile, as Salomon has argued [154], burdens depressed the producing classes. It has been usual to talk of a freer peasantry in Catalonia after the Sentence of Guadalupe of 1486, but there too the changes were not favourable [155] and the lot of the poorer peasants worsened. Thus the position of the rural classes in early modern Spain seems to have been aggravated on one hand by an unprogressive agricultural system, on the other by a restricting social environment: this situation, of course, was common throughout southern Europe and the Mediterranean.

The agrarian crisis, when it came after the 1580s, could be seen in: a fall in wheat production (by at least a third, and often much more); a decline in rental income (in Segovia landlords complained of falls of 50 per cent); a shrinkage of arable; a decrease in livestock (the flocks of the Mesta, Klein shows, fell from some three million head in the sixteenth century to two million in the seventeenth); and a levelling-off in commodity and food prices, which however maintained their upward trend because of monetary inflation. The contraction also occurred in other countries, but the impact on Spain was arguably more severe, with no evidence that structural changes occurred as a result of the crisis, leading Casey to conclude that 'Spain's peculiar failure was an inability to complete the transition to a more urbanised economy' [125], a transition that nations in northern Europe were successfully making. The crisis that afflicted Castile at the very height of its imperial power has received special attention from Castilian scholars in the last few years, who have attempted to set in perspective the very many factors involved [156].

The pastoral economy has been little studied. Livestock (cattle, sheep, pigs, goats) was crucial to the rural economy; sheep were particularly important, being the mainstay of the cottage and textile industry (in its main centres at Segovia, Toledo and Cuenca), and also of the export trade; there was therefore good reason to maintain extensive pasture. However, a long historiographical tradition dating from the eighteenth century has given a continuously bad press to the sheepowners' guild, the Mesta [157], by attributing many of the failings of the economy to the pastoral interest. Vassberg summarises the findings of modern scholarship when he states that 'some historians have concluded that early modern Spanish agriculture was ruined by depredations of migratory flocks. That is simply not true' [151].

Given the predominance of the agrarian sector in all pre-industrial economies, it is obvious that the industrial sector was small. In Spain this was particularly so, both because of a lack of resources and because the markets were small and regionalised in a country which had no unified political structure. Only fragmentary information is available on pre-eighteenth-century industry, but it appears that the main textile areas in the mid-sixteenth century were Segovia (the most important for woollens), Granada (silk), Toledo (silk and woollens) and Cuenca (woollens). In line with demographic growth and agricultural expansion in the late fifteenth century there appears to have been a notable increase in textile output, on the evidence from Cuenca [158]. Side by side with this domestic industry, however, there had existed since the later Middle Ages an active export trade of quality wool (the merino sheep) and silk from Granada. Well into the sixteenth century the right of domestic manufacturers to at least a third of raw materials was guaranteed by public authority. By then, however, the international economic situation had changed, and foreigners who bought Spanish raw materials were turning them into quality manufactured goods and sending these back into Spain at competitive prices. Spain's soaring inflation, and consequent higher production costs, helped to make the foreign textiles relatively cheaper; moreover, foreign manufacturers were even more encouraged to export to Spain by the possibility of being paid in American bullion. Thus Spain's domestic industry faced difficult times. Some internal developments made the situation worse: in Granada, for example, the old Moorish textile industry was slowly crushed by non-Morisco speculators who cornered raw silk production and sought good prices from foreign buyers. Commentators and members of the Cortes, particularly in the seventeenth century, asked for protectionist measures such as a ban on the export of bullion and of raw materials, but these were unrealistic demands that would also have had negative effects on Spain. The textile industry had a moment of glory in the boom of the sixteenth century, when production at Segovia by 1585 attained levels comparable to famous centres such as Florence, but soon many merchants were getting better returns from exporting wool than from selling it to Spanish factories. Figures for cloth production tell plainly the sad story of a fragile domestic textile industry that recovered slightly during the early eighteenth century but in general remained depressed until the nineteenth.

The influence of international trade. The commercial links of the peninsula were a crucial aspect of the ups and downs in its economy. The wool trade was fundamental and played a key role in the growth of Spain's financial market, centred during the early sixteenth century in the northern towns of Burgos and Medina del Campo, with good access to the trading ports of Bilbao and Santander. Since foreign merchants were those primarily interested in the trade, the business life of these towns had a truly cosmopolitan air, and thanks to Lapeyre's studies of the Ruiz family [159] we know a good deal about the functioning and difficulties of trade at that time. The decay of the fairs of northern Castile after the 1570s, provoked to a great extent by the disturbances in the important market of the Netherlands, was the prelude to a restructuring of the Castilian economy, for precisely at this period large sections of the peninsula were benefiting from the discovery of America [160]. The middle years of the sixteenth century were a boom period in which the success story of the Castilian fairs overlapped with the new wealth of Seville and Andalusia, bringing a sensation of well-being to a country that had enjoyed peace for half a century. Moreover, in 1561 Philip II made Madrid his permanent capital, and the town slowly began to expand, creating a booming economy of its own. These developments of course had their negative side: the decay of the fairs at Medina del Campo and the shift of the capital from Valladolid moved the centre of activity away from northern Castile, and the great cities there, from Burgos to Toledo, suffered decline and shrank to the level of quiet provincial towns. 'Without the court here, this town is solitary and poor', wrote a Jesuit from Valladolid in 1570.

The predominance of both Seville and Madrid calls for comment. Seville's dual role in the national and the international economy is complex and has not hitherto invited the attentions of any scholar, beyond the multi-volume study of its commerce done by Pierre Chaunu in the 1960s. The city grew in size from about 7000 households in the 1480s to over 10 000 in 1533 and about 24 000 in the 1590s, remaining steady at this level until the numbers were severely cut by the epidemic of 1649 to about 16 250 households [161]. It functioned chiefly as: an outlet to America of produce from southern Spain; a port of receipt for the bullion and produce of America; a centre for international traders who dealt in these two trades; and an outlet for emigration to the New World. The economic activity of Seville certainly helped to regenerate many sectors of the economy in the mid-sixteenth century, and continued for long thereafter to stimulate sectors such as shipbuilding. However, the growing incapacity of Spanish industry to supply America with manufactured goods meant that the gap was quickly filled by foreign traders and their agents resident in Seville, where the foreign colony soon dominated the social and cultural life of the city. Seville's success has therefore been seen as a symbol of the 'dependence' of the Spanish economy on outside producers. From the 1580s, commentators in Castile began to denounce the mechanics of the monopoly system, which effectively worked in favour of foreign finance. Figures for the period show clearly that Seville was no longer really a Spanish port: most of the goods traded out were foreign, and most of that coming in from America went to foreigners [162].

The case of Madrid, studied in detail by Ringrose, offers a parallel example of the negative consequences exercised by a major city over its dependent regions. Whereas a capital like London has been seen by historians as a stimulant to its hinterland, Ringrose sees post-1561 Madrid as a parasite, absorbing population and produce from its surrounding areas but in no real way aiding their growth; the capital 'could provide little stimulus for interior Spain, and may have functioned as a motor for regional economic stagnation' [163]. His thesis is suggestive, and renders the valuable service of looking at the capital within its regional context rather than within the misleading context of the nation; it adds material, moreover, to the debate over 'decline'.

The key role of Madrid and Seville derived in part from their link with international trade [164]. Castile had not been a notable seafaring nation in the later Middle Ages; only the Basques had an active history of seagoing. Catalonia, by contrast, was forced by its environment towards the sea, and thus had a background not only of imperial expansion in the Mediterranean but also of regular trade with Italy. The greater volume of economic power in the peninsula, however, was Castilian, and it is fundamentally the trade of Castile that historians have chosen to study. By the fifteenth century there is ample evidence of the dedication of Castilians to trade with their neighbours, so there can be no foundation for the assumption that Castilians were somehow non-capitalistic. But it is undeniable that Castilian unfamiliarity with the sea meant that much marine trade was transported not by Castilians but by foreigners (English, Dutch, French), who continued throughout the early modern period to dominate the carrying trade, with negative consequences for Spanish economic autonomy. In 1503 the Venetian ambassador, commenting on the influence of Genoese merchants, claimed that 'one third of Genoa is in Spain'. By the seventeenth century, the bulk of shipping in Spanish ports was foreign, and there were major commercial centres (such as Alicante) where transport was almost 100 per cent in foreign vessels. Thus analysis of Spanish port statistics (there are studies for Seville, Bilbao, Barcelona) can be deceptive. Normally, for instance, an increase in port traffic would suggest an improvement in the regional economy, but in Spain it more likely proves that the economy was being depressed even further by foreign imports. Spanish trade data are hard to find and need to be treated with great caution: an obvious example is the Indies trade operated from Seville and Cadiz, where the official figures are often falsified and misleading.

The important role of American bullion in the economic evolution both of Spain and of Europe was used by Pierre Chaunu as a backcloth for his argument that the movements of shipping across the Atlantic coincided with the rise and fall both of prices and of bullion imports. This picture not only confirmed the schema of a 'decline' in Spain in the seventeenth century, it also coincided with the argument of many French historians that the expansion of the sixteenth century ended around 1620, and that a depression set into the European economy from the mid-century. However, subsequent work by Everaert [162], Kamen [252] and especially Morineau [165], all of them working not on official Spanish returns (which were Hamilton's source) but on the reports of foreign consuls in Seville and Cadiz, has demonstrated that bullion imports from America did not decline during the seventeenth century but rose to unprecedented levels. This conclusion overturns older preconceptions not only on 'decline' but also on the alleged deceleration of the European economy. Little bullion entered the peninsula – it was mostly re-exported both from Spain and from

Europe [129] – but what did may have helped to stabilise prices. Work on the question has helped to fix attention on the major role of American silver in the evolution of both the peninsular and the world economy.

The economic recovery of the seventeenth century. The economic difficulties of Spain, aggravated by its imperial commitments, have led many historians to consider the entire seventeenth century as a period of profound decay. More recently, it has been argued that the problems were part of a structural crisis rather than a 'decline', were concentrated in the last decade of the sixteenth and the first half of the seventeenth century, and that from the 1660s there were signs of renewal in vital sectors [166]. The evidence has been summarised by Pere Molas [167], though significant exceptions to a picture of recovery can always be found, because of the variety in Spain's regional economies. Given the important variations between regions and sectors, it is obvious that words like 'decline' and 'recovery' have little meaning when applied to the whole country. What then was the situation after the period of crisis? Briefly, in population we can say that the northwest (Galicia, Asturias, the Basque country) maintained its levels without interruption, and all the eastern periphery (Catalonia, Valencia, Murcia) showed clear expansion after the 1660s. Casey has cautiously described the evolution of Valencia in the whole century as 'a long depopulation', but the indications from a study of parish records in Guadalest [168], where an annual growth rate of 2.2 per cent could be found after the 1660s, suggest a rapid and remarkable population recovery. In Old Castile, there was an unmistakable but slow upturn. By contrast, in the whole crescent of southwest Spain (Extremadura, some of New Castile, Andalusia) recovery was hampered by the Portuguese wars and by the epidemics of 1676–85. On balance, and given the exceptions, the rise in the birth rate after 1660 is indisputable; but in perspective the population rise of the late century was little more than a partial recovery of lost ground, so that demographers who consider the whole century to be one of negative growth and decline are also correct.

Despite this equivocal situation, production levels per unit farmed rose in most of Spain from the 1660s. It has been suggested, as we have seen, that this was because farmers were now, with fewer mouths to feed, cultivating only the better lands. During the same period, there is scattered evidence that livestock levels rose as well. In both demography and output, then, the late seventeenth century was – given the obvious exceptions – a period of hope, whose positive aspects were not confirmed until the next generation. However, the textile industry remained depressed and only a slight rise in output was registered at Segovia: the hopeful sign here was that the government from the 1670s encouraged investment through committees for trade (Juntas de Comercio) [169]. Trade remained firmly in foreign hands, and the decay of Seville during this period was a prelude to the meteoric rise from 1681 of Cadiz, which thereafter became the principal port for American trade. In brief, there was undoubted recovery both in Castile and in the Mediterranean in the vital sectors (population, agriculture and livestock) but in dependent sectors (industry, commerce), more closely related to the European trade pattern, there was little. Thus the economic recuperation of Spain in the seventeenth century was, like its boom in the sixteenth, flawed by basic structural weaknesses.

In terms of the Spanish economy, the following contrast between the epochs of alleged success and alleged decline gives food for thought. In 1590 the Spain of Philip II was supposed to be still at the peak of its power, and in 1690 the Spain of Charles II was supposed to be at the depth of its alleged decline. Yet, in 1590 population was falling, and in 1690 it was rising. In 1590 agriculture was stagnating, in 1690 it was booming. In 1590 silver imports from America were falling, in 1690 they had never been higher. In 1590 inflation was soaring, in 1690 it had come to an end. In 1590 the state budget was in ruins, in 1690 the government was reducing taxes. In 1590 Spain was spending its income and men on wars, in 1690 there were few major war fronts. At virtually every point, the governing elites and traders of Spain were preparing themselves with optimism for a good future.

5 Why was there no Reformation?

Cultural minorities and the impact of expulsion. Why was there no Reformation? What was the role of the Counter-Reformation? Why was there an Inquisition? Did the Holy Office destroy freedom?

The coexistence of three major religions – Islam, Christianity and Judaism – in the peninsula for some seven centuries had a formative influence on the character of Spain and has coloured its literature and history. Interpretations of Spanish culture have never been lacking. For many scholars Spain is 'different' to an extent that requires special categories and a special type of explanation (see also Chapter 6). Because of the Muslim heritage in the south of the peninsula, some have felt that in culture it is closer to Africa than to western Europe. In the past century, Américo Castro's views on the subject have been very influential, mainly in the United States [170]. He argued that the Arabs and above all the Jews bequeathed to Spain powerful creative traditions that have endured to our own day. His 'oriental interpretation' was sharply attacked from all sides, notably by the medieval historian Claudio Sánchez Albornoz [171], but has served to stimulate debate. Taken together with some older opinions about Spaniards (their alleged non-capitalist mentality, for example), these theories present Spain as a nation with attitudes distinct from those found in the rest of Europe. More recent scholars (notably J. A. Maravall) have insisted by contrast that Spain was not as isolated from the Western tradition as has been believed.

It is a common misapprehension to believe that coexistence ('convivencia') between the three religions of the peninsula created a tolerant people. Of necessity the Christians, Muslims and

Jews borrowed from each other in dress, language and customs, because living side by side for over five hundred years was not a short-term exercise. The cultural interchange has left an enduring imprint on the Spanish character and landscape. However, coexistence was accompanied by periods of war, massacre and oppression. Jews were always a disadvantaged minority under the two other religions, while Christians nurtured a fierce hostility to Islam that survived in the ten-year war (1482–92) to free Granada from Muslim rule. When the Inquisition was created by Christians in the fifteenth century it was inevitable that it should direct its pressure against people of Jewish and Muslim origin rather than look for dissent among its own adherents.

Cultural minorities and the impact of expulsion. From being a society with experience of *convivencia*, early modern Spain became a persecuting society because of the problems that resulted from trying to integrate former Muslims and Jews into the Christian fold. It was the only Western nation to take this path, with enduring consequences for Spanish character and culture. In 1492 Ferdinand and Isabella followed the advice of the Inquisition and issued a decree offering all the Jews of Spain the choice between conversion and expulsion. Because the king and queen were by no means anti-Semitic (many of their advisers, secretaries, financiers and doctors were either Jews or *conversos*) the decree should be seen as a religious rather than a racialist move. The famous 'expulsion' of the Jews was carried out in the summer of 1492 [172]. Figures upwards of 150 000 have often been suggested for those expelled; but when we bear in mind that the decree aimed at *conversion* rather than expulsion, that the Jews were in any case a tiny minority after the forced conversions of the previous century, and that very many returned to Spain after leaving it in the 1490s, it is logical to suggest that the real total emigration was not more than about 50 000 out of a total Jewish population in Spain of around 100 000 [173]. The economic repercussions were negligible, since Jews played a marginal role in Christian society, but there were serious cultural consequences. Those who stayed behind and got baptised were known as *conversos*; their numbers were added to the many other *conversos* who had been baptised by force in late medieval times. Forming virtually a society within a society, they were resented by non-Jewish Spaniards and their religious practice was looked upon with suspicion. Many modern scholars have debated the question 'What was the true religion of the *conversos*?' [174]. A dozen years before the 'expulsion' of the Jews, this question had provoked the establishment of an Inquisition [175] and was in reality the direct cause of the expulsion itself, since the Inquisition felt that getting rid of Jews would encourage *conversos* to reject Judaism and be true Christians.

The persecution of Jews was in numerical terms a small matter compared to what the Muslims of Spain experienced. In late medieval Spain – notably in Valencia – the Muslims had lived in conditions of tolerable *convivencia* with Christians [176]. When the kingdom of Granada capitulated to Ferdinand and Isabella they promised to respect the Islamic religion of the inhabitants, but in 1500 the queen ordered the Muslims of the Crown of Castile to convert to Christianity, and a quarter of a century later (1526) her grandson Charles V accepted a similar decision for the Muslims of the Crown of Aragon. The 'converts' were known as Moriscos, who invariably lived apart from Christians and continued to practice their old religion openly. It was a situation that bred mutual intolerance and perennial conflict [177]. After the great Morisco rising of 1570 in the kingdom of Granada, when Muslims from Africa and Turkey helped the insurgents, there was little doubt about the outcome. In 1609–14 the Spanish government carried out a massive expulsion of virtually the entire Islamic population of Spain, nearly 300 000 people [178]. It was the biggest act of deportation carried out till that time in Europe's history. This time the consequences were clearly negative, especially in provinces (such as Valencia) where the Moriscos had been a majority. But in no way did the expulsions cause any serious or long-range harm to Spain's economy, since the Moriscos (like the Jews before them) did not form an integral part of the country's systems of production.

The two famous expulsions have left the permanent stamp of religious intolerance on Spain, and have consequently given rise to widely differing explanations of why they happened. The conservative school has tried to defend Spain's position, arguing that the conversos were a 'danger' to the purity of the Catholic faith, and that the Moriscos were a permanent threat to national security. Others, such as Fernand Braudel, have seen in the expulsions a profound 'clash between civilizations'. Braudel's study on *The Mediterranean* is essentially the narrative of a struggle between

Christians and Muslims that came to a head at the naval battle of Lepanto in 1571. The expulsions left Christianity as the only officially recognised religion in Spain, a situation that brought the country into line with the rest of western Europe.

Why was there no Reformation in Spain? The spiritual and Church history of the Golden Age is heavily affected by the absence of any development in Spain along the lines of the Protestant Reformation [179]. It is sometimes suggested that there was no Reformation because there was no need for one, since Ferdinand and Isabella reformed the Church. The claim is wholly untrue. The Catholic Monarchs tried to reform a couple of religious orders in central Castile, and appointed a handful of pious bishops; but they left untouched every aspect of the institutions, ritual, clergy and religious life of the people throughout Spain. The Church remained as unreformed as anywhere else in Europe. No effective moves for change were made until the 1560s, when Philip II personally took an interest in the question and Spain became the first European country to impose the decrees of the Council of Trent [180].

In elite circles, of course, there had long been reformist ideas. From the Netherlands some clergy received the influence of spiritual movements (the *'devotio moderna'*) and of Erasmus. Erasmian humanism did not enjoy wide support in Spain [181]; it was essentially a 'court' movement, and its high tide (1520–30) coincided almost exactly with Charles V's first stay in Spain. Meanwhile the Spaniards who accompanied Charles V to Germany in 1520 had met Luther and admired him. But most of them eventually rejected the new tendencies, which failed to penetrate Spain. The government issued one decree against Luther's works in 1525, yet no other was deemed necessary for a quarter of a century. The failure of heresy to penetrate the peninsula at a time when it was spreading all over western Europe remains a puzzle. Why did Protestantism strike no roots in Spain for a generation? Why was it easy to eliminate when discovered? One suggestion made is that Spaniards were (unlike other Europeans) solidly Catholic and could not be subverted. The testimony of missionaries in the peninsula in the late sixteenth century, however, demonstrates that Spaniards were by no means solid in their religious grounding. Another suggestion is that fear of the Inquisition 'froze Spain into orthodoxy' (the phrase was coined by J. L. Motley) [113]. In fact, there was very little cause for fear. In the thirty years that followed the decree of 1525, the Inquisition took no special measures against foreign heresy, burnt perhaps one alleged 'Lutheran', and the famous *auto de fe* virtually disappeared from sight. In those thirty years foreign books entered the peninsula with impunity, and no censorship controls were applied.

It is hence not easy to give a convincing answer to the puzzle. One must certainly reject the picture of a wholly Catholic nation that refused to countenance error. The most likely explanation for the failure of Lutheranism to penetrate, is that the multicultural scenario of *convivencia* offered so much confrontation with Judaism and Islam that it allowed little scope for dissent within the Christian body. In the Middle Ages Castile had been, for the same reason, virtually free of identifiable heresy. The absence of native dissent offered no basis for heterodoxy to build on, unlike England where the Reformation could build on Lollardy. When dissent did arise, it was among those who were the principal heirs to a multicultural background: the *conversos* of Jewish origin. Quite significantly, in the 1530s the Inquisition in Castile was absorbed not with Germanic heresy but with the religious groups known as 'alumbrados', most of them of converso origin [182], who in some measure prepared the way for neo-Protestant groups that sprang up in Castile and Andalusia. Not until 1558 were Protestant cells discovered in Castile [183]. However, few heretics were identified, and Spain strangely enough executed fewer religious dissidents in the era of the Reformation than any other country of western Europe.

What was the role of the Counter-Reformation? Spaniards have traditionally believed that the Counter-Reformation (the sixteenth-century reform movement inspired from within the Catholic Church and directed in part against the Reformation) happened only outside Spain, not inside it. It has consequently been easy to accept the image of a firmly Catholic country where nothing changed over the centuries. Church history written by Spaniards limited itself to what happened inside the religious orders. Historians in France and Italy, however, were discovering a generation ago that the study of pastoral visits made by bishops could throw light on the real state of everyday religion. From the 1980s,

historians of Spain began to use diocesan papers, testaments and
Inquisition documents to arrive at an understanding of peninsular
Catholicism. There is now no doubt that a substantial Counter
Reformation occurred in Spain [184]. From at least the 1480s,
some Church leaders were anxious to improve the state of religious knowledge and practice among their people, and around
1510 Dominican friars were active as missionaries in northern
Spain. However, no significant push for reform occurred before
1565, when Philip II formally received the decrees of the Council
of Trent and supervised the holding of provincial councils of the
clergy. The date marks the beginning of the Counter-Reformation
in Spain. The king, who insisted that all aspects of the programme
should be under Spanish control, had two main objectives: to
improve the quality of the clergy and convert the people to true
religion. To help him in his goal he enlisted the Inquisition (which
from this date began to look closely at the day-to-day religious and
moral practice of Spaniards) and invited new religious orders from
Italy (the Jesuits and Capuchins, among others) to enter the country and preach sermons. The Jesuit order had been founded by a
Basque noble, Ignatius Loyola, and though many Spaniards came
to play a prominent part in it the order was always essentially an
international one, independent of Spanish control.

A serious attempt was made to improve the quality of the bishops and clergy. Rules of celibacy and enclosure were enforced, and
seminaries were founded to train priests [185]. In everyday religion there were revolutionary innovations: the form of the mass
was altered, thousands of new churches were built, pulpits and
confessionals were set up for the first time, new devotions (such as
the rosary) were introduced, the rules of marriage were changed,
and lay associations (known as confraternities) [186] were set up
in each parish. At the same time traditional community acts, such
as processions and festivities, were put under clerical control. The
reforms tried to give a unique role to male clergy, especially to
the person of the parish priest; by contrast, women were allotted a
secondary role in all Church activities.

There was certainly an impact, as we can see from the strong
opposition among both clergy and people, but it remains open to
debate whether the changes were effective and lasting, and much
of the initial impetus for reform disappeared in little more than a
generation. Outside the main towns, it is likely that old-time forms

of religion continued without change. In pre-industrial society, 'religion' did not imply only the Church but also included elements of customary folklore and community practice. The Church, indeed, played a relatively small part in the lives of country people, who occupied their time in a broad range of activities rooted in their traditions. The Counter-Reformation probably had small impact on this 'popular religion', which differed in content from one locality to the next, adopted its own local preferences in saints, and even insisted on having local versions of the Virgin Mary [187]. It has been suggested that knowledge of basic religion improved [188], but the claim is not statistically reliable and refers only to one town, Toledo.

During these decades the Spanish Church was also active in the Spanish empire [189]. It is however a fundamental mistake to assume that the activity of the Church overseas was in some way a projection of the Counter-Reformation Church in the peninsula. In reality, most of the pioneering enterprises of Spanish clergy overseas had taken place by the 1560s, well before the era of the Counter-Reformation in the peninsula. After the 1570s, the nature of the missionary impulse in the colonies changed, and the Jesuits played a more prominent role.

The study of popular religion has opened up the debate over whether Spain in the age of the Reformation was really Catholic. The traditional picture was of a firmly Catholic country that stoutly resisted the Reformation and rejected the Jews and Moriscos. Research into religious practice and belief, especially in the rural and mountainous regions of Spain, reveals that on the contrary Catholicism was often little more than a veneer on popular practices. An interesting example is the prevalence of the opinion, actively pursued by the Inquisition in a few areas during the early modern period, that sexual intercourse ('fornication') between unmarried adults was not sinful [190]. It is also apparent that hostility to the cultural minorities was not always as profound as official propaganda pretended, and that a practical tolerance could often be found not only at the elite level but also among sections of the population [191]. Like other countries, Spain appears to have had its share of unbelievers and half-believers, whose way of thinking did not always follow the official line. This complex picture inevitably had much to do with regional differences within Spain, since contact with exterior cultures (with Muslims in

Andalusia, for example, or with French in Catalonia) gave people a broader vision of social relations. The social study of religion, in brief, illuminates the surprising richness of attitudes that underlay the official postulates of belief during the Golden Age.

A recurring aspect of popular religion was the belief in witchcraft, which during the early modern period was fiercely persecuted in most countries and took a heavy toll in the lives of witches punished. To deal with problems such as illness, epidemics and adverse weather, where the Church could offer no solution, people resorted to remedies that might be religious in appearance but contained aspects that the clergy denounced as 'superstition'. Non-official remedies were often looked upon as diabolic 'witchcraft', and persecuted by the authorities. The Spanish Inquisition played a part in prosecuting the phenomenon, but its role was surprisingly enlightened, for it insisted that 'witchcraft' was imaginary and therefore not a criminal offence. Whereas in most other countries witches were executed, the Spanish clergy (like those of Italy) refused to treat their offence as heresy, and clear directives from the Inquisition in 1526 and in 1610 made sure that the burning of witches was virtually unknown. However, the secular authorities in Spain continued to execute witches (by hanging), and the number of their victims may have been substantial [192].

Why was there an Inquisition? The Inquisition, established by Ferdinand and Isabella in 1480, continues to excite controversy [193]. There had been local Inquisitions in other parts of Europe in medieval times, but the Spanish tribunal is the most notorious [194]. From the fourteenth century the Crown of Aragon had links with the papal Inquisition in France, by contrast Castile had never had a general tribunal to deal with heresy, an offence that bishops had normally dealt with in their courts. The new tribunal of 1480 soon extended its authority over both Castile and Aragon. Its express purpose was to deal with the religious practices of the 'conversos' of Jewish origin. Virtually all the people it arrested and examined in the first thirty years of its existence were conversos, a fact that has excited controversy among Jewish scholars. One school of thought feels that the Inquisition had good reasons for acting as it did because all the conversos were authentic Jews [195]. A dissenting view, pioneered by Netanyahu, holds that on the contrary the conversos were authentic Christians, persecuted not for their beliefs but for their ethnic origins. Netanyahu also feels that the Inquisition was a tool used by Ferdinand to advance royal absolute power [196]. Non-Jewish historians tend not to accept either of these interpretations without qualification.

Disagreement about the Inquisition has usually extended to all areas of its activity. Apart from its persecution of Jewish conversos, it attended to a broad range of questions until its final suppression in 1834. Commentators used to consider it a bloodthirsty institution, but that view can rightly be discarded. Thousands of conversos were certainly arrested in the early years, but few were imprisoned and even fewer executed. The repression of those early decades, never to be repeated in the remaining 300 years of the Inquisition's existence, cost the lives of possibly 2000 conversos, a fraction of the figure advanced by some writers. Nevertheless, exaggeration of the Inquisition's role and impact remains difficult to avoid. Although a large amount of research into the tribunal has been done in recent decades, it has failed to undermine the conviction of those who feel that the Inquisition 'must have' had a larger role than the facts indicate. This makes it inevitable that popular opinion will continue to exaggerate or sensationalise the role of the tribunal, and ignore research based on the documents.

The problem with research is that it uses sources that are sometimes tainted and make sense only when viewed in context. Moreover, accepting what the documents say often means accepting what the inquisitors say, and their criteria were not necessarily reliable. A recent attempt to convert the Inquisitorial case documents into statistics [197], has collapsed because the statistics turned out to be seriously deficient and no acceptable conclusions could be drawn from them. In the same way, exclusive reliance on the same papers can draw us into the trap of seeing events principally from the viewpoint of the inquisitors. This may lead us to exaggerate the role in society of a tribunal that, seen from a broader perspective, often had little part to play in the daily lives of Spaniards. There is, certainly, no evidence that the tribunal ever acted as a tool of 'social control'. The inquisitors limited their activities to the main urban centres, neglecting almost entirely the small towns and the countryside, where most people lived. In the heart of Castile, in Toledo, five times as many townspeople as peasants were tried by the tribunal [198]. The evidence for Catalonia is incontrovertible: 'in over 90 per cent of the towns, during more than three centuries of existence, the Holy Office never once intruded' [180; p. 436]. In Galicia the tribunal was almost unknown, functioning in the diocese of Ourense, according to Allyson Poska, 'for a total of only 16 months during the entire seventeenth century' [184; p. 7]. The situation was clearly the same elsewhere in Spain, and deflates any idea of the tribunal exercising 'social control'.

Despite its low profile, the Inquisition provoked considerable opposition from many social sectors, from competing jurisdictions and from bishops and clergy. Analysis of this opposition has helped us to understand from the inside how some opposition groups functioned. The best analysis of this problem of the relationship between inquisitors and the society in which they lived, has been done for medieval Languedoc, where there was a French Inquisition [199]. A similar analysis could undoubtedly be done for Spain [200]. The tribunal certainly received more support within the kingdoms of Castile than it did in the other realms of the monarchy, where local privileges fought hard and often successfully against the introduction of a foreign institution that clashed with the interests of both the elites and the clergy [201].

Did the Holy Office destroy freedom? The time-honoured view, disseminated by Protestant writers and nineteenth-century scholars, was that the Inquisition extinguished freedom and destroyed Spain's culture. The view continues to be held by many who believe that the tribunal 'must have' done so. Verisimilitude is added to the view by another common argument: since Spain had an undeveloped economy and also lagged behind in scientific matters, the Inquisition must have caused it. The permanent utility of the Inquisition is that it can be blamed for everything. It was an attitude to be found in much of Europe in the later sixteenth century, when every other nation was in conflict with Spain and identified the Holy Office as the source of all ills. Some conservative Spaniards in the twentieth century in self-defence referred to the hostile propaganda as a 'Black Legend', but of course, it was not all legend.

The theme provokes continuing debate and because of its ideological implications will never be satisfactorily resolved. It is common to assert (against all the known facts) that the Inquisition controlled Spain. Already in the sixteenth century the Venetian ambassadors to Spain maintained that all Spaniards lived in fear of the tribunal, which (they said) even controlled the king. Other contemporaries testified that Spaniards were not allowed to write or even think freely. Did the Inquisition repress thought? The problem of censorship is one of the crucial points at which the whole problem can be examined [202]. The contrast of opinions on the matter is striking. One view, strongly supported by conservative Spaniards, denies any negative influence. The nineteenth-century writer Menéndez y Pelayo asserted that 'never was there more written in Spain, or better written, than in the two golden centuries of the Inquisition'. By contrast, Américo Castro claimed that 'not to think or learn or read' became habitual for Spaniards faced by 'the sadism and lust for plunder of those of the Holy Office'.

What was the real impact of book control? The overall impact of systems of literary censorship is difficult to judge. Though it is widely believed that Spanish literature suffered at the hands of the Inquisition, there are good reasons to question the belief. First, most Western countries had a comparable system of control, yet none appears to have suffered significantly [203]. Book control and censorship were systematically evaded in all countries where practised, and Spain was no exception. Second, prohibited books had a negligible readership in the peninsula. Most banned books were in foreign languages, never even remotely in reach of the Spanish reader, and never available in the peninsula. Third, those who really wished to obtain banned books of special interest – in astrology, medicine, scholarship – faced few obstacles. They brought books in personally, or through commercial channels, or asked friends abroad to send them. Total freedom of movement between the peninsula and France and Italy, guaranteed an unimpeded circulation of people, books and – at one remove – ideas. Finally, no evidence has ever emerged that the book controls harmed thought. The bulk of creative literature available to Spaniards never appeared in the Index. Up to the mid-sixteenth century, the Inquisition played no significant part in the literary world, prosecuted no notable writer, and interfered substantially only with some texts of Renaissance theatre [204]. The Inquisition's overseeing of literature, in short, looked imposing in theory but was unimpressive in practice. In the seventeenth century, the Index had a limited, even petty role. The conclusion holds not only for books by native Spanish authors, but also for foreign writers. If ordinary Spaniards did not read foreign authors it was for the very same reason that prevails today: the books were not available in Spanish, or were too specialised for their tastes.

It is commonly assumed that when Philip II returned to Spain in 1559 he sealed the country off from foreign influences. Since the king never had the means to do so, the assumption makes no sense, and the objective could never have been achieved, for during the age of empire Spaniards were the most travelled nation in the world, including in their orbit not only the whole of Europe but also the New World and Asia. It is sometimes also affirmed that in 1559 the government 'forbade Spanish students to go abroad for study' [7; p. 225]. No such prohibition was ever issued. Castilian students always remained free to go abroad to the colleges that they had frequented, and though they were forbidden to go elsewhere they often did not observe the edict. Long after the law of 1559, Catholic Spaniards could be found studying in France, the Netherlands and Germany. Meanwhile, students in the rest of Spain went where they wished and suffered no restrictions until the end of the century.

Moreover, there is no sign whatever of any restriction on personal and commercial links with Italy (nearly half of which was within the Spanish empire) [205], and links with the Netherlands though sometimes interrupted by war were never cut. These two nations continued to enjoy a lasting and profound relationship with the Iberian peninsula, as we can see by their close commercial, financial, artistic and intellectual links [206]. Just as the military capacity of Spain was enhanced by its confederates within the multiple monarchy, so the cultural creativity of the Golden Age drew on much foreign inspiration and was not exclusively Hispanic. The deep debt to Italy of Spanish art, poetry and music is too well known to need comment. These close international links nevertheless remained ambivalent. Italians, for example, had good political reasons for distrusting Spain, and the comments of both their ambassadors and their distinguished visitors (both nobles and prelates) were uniformly hostile. The relative isolation of Spain, then, seems to owe less to the existence of censorship than to political tensions. A typical case is that of relations with France. Spaniards read and admired Bodin and Montaigne in translation, published their own books freely in

French territory (in the late sixteenth and early seventeenth century over one hundred Spanish authors had their works printed in Lyon, without any criticism from the Spanish authorities), and those who could read the language purchased French books avidly [207]; none of this ever dispelled the element of distrust.

The active cultural links of Spain need emphasising, in view of the still prevailing impression that the peninsula was in some way culturally strangled. Technical backwardness (rather than religious repression) was, as scholars have convincingly shown, one of the reasons why publishing never became big business in the peninsula. Without any sophisticated printing presses of its own, Spain was obliged to resort to the printers of Antwerp and of Lyon, and thanks to this managed to maintain an effective literary output throughout the early modern period [208]. Censorship may have had a restricting effect [209], as it had in every European country, but the prohibitions of the famous inquisitorial Indices of the sixteenth century applied overwhelmingly to foreign-language books that had never been within the reach of Spaniards anyway.

6 Was Spain 'different'?: Society and Culture in the Golden Age

Was Spain 'different'? Were Spaniards hostile to capitalism? The relevance of the notions of 'honour' and 'purity of blood'. Were women disadvantaged in society? Were the nobility idle and the peasants hardworking? Problems of wealth and poverty in traditional society.

For non-Spaniards the particular appeal of Spain has been its exotic nature. Among Americans, Washington Irving depicted the delights of the Alhambra and Hemingway celebrated the cult of the bull. Bizet's opera *Carmen* popularised a specific vision of how Spaniards were thought to be. For their part, many Spaniards (mainly Castilians) did not feel attracted to the world outside and tended to reject it, sheltering being the idea that they were different. The notion of 'difference' was seized on with enthusiasm both in Spain and outside, by scholars who found it a useful way of studying Spanish culture. But it may also be a barrier to understanding.

Was Spain 'different'? The theory of isolation from western society, configuring Spain as an 'African' and not a 'European' country, was based on two main ideas: its multicultural experience down to the end of the Reconquest era (twelfth century), and its apparent separation from European currents from the reign of Philip II (sixteenth century) onwards. Because Spain seemed to have a separate development in both mediaeval and modern times, some writers maintained that Spain had no proper Renaissance, no authentic Baroque and no Counter-Reformation. The notion of 'difference', however, goes further. Certain social characteristics–intense religious zeal, entrenched concepts of honour – were and are viewed as being peculiarly Spanish and rooted in the history of Spaniards. Both socially and culturally the nation was thought of as a world apart. This isolationist vision can be found among writers of all persuasions. It has attracted conservative traditionalists because it emphasises what are seen as authentic 'Spanish' values. It has appealed to non-Spaniards because it confirms the romantic image of a nation living in the past. And it has been exploited by 'liberal' Spaniards in order to suggest an alternative approach to the problems of their country.

The richness of Spain's experience confirms that it would be misleading to write of the culture and society of the Golden Age only in terms of 'the Castilian mind' [210]. Spain was more than Castile. Castilian printed books certainly dominated the peninsular market from the sixteenth century onwards, but in a society where illiteracy was extremely high, the daily life of Spaniards has to be defined in terms not only of what they read but also of what they did with their time. The dominance of Castilian books in the bookshops of Catalonia, for example, had a minimal impact on the everyday culture of Catalans. Recent study of the contact-point between elite and popular cultures, particularly in the theatre and in public leisure activities, has confirmed that Spanish society was rich and complex, and that an attempt to study it only through the eyes of Castilian literature does not illuminate all aspects of experience in the peninsula [211].

Were Spaniards hostile to capitalism? Despite the continuous participation of Spaniards in trade, industry and agriculture in early modern times, some historians have felt that they were anti-capitalist in spirit. Attempting to explain why Spanish traders were unable to benefit from their nation's favourable economic position in the sixteenth century, Fernand Braudel [2] proposed the notable thesis of a 'betrayal by the bourgeoisie', according to which those who were active in trade withdrew their money once they had made their fortunes, and thereby prejudiced the chance of further capitalist investment. In other words, they allowed a dominant social prejudice against moneymaking to influence their economic activity. Few historians now take this view. The competence of Spaniards – not only Catalans and Basques but also Castilians – as capitalists during the early modern period has been firmly stressed by several recent writers [212], and there is substantial evidence of Castilians in international trade in the sixteenth century [213].

Two specific problems, those of investment and status, merit comment. The presence or absence of a strong native capitalist sector depended obviously on opportunities for investment. We might expect to find the sector in a protected wool market (Burgos) or an average regional port (Barcelona), but the sector might not be strong in a big international port with heavy competition (Seville). The evolution of a capitalist sector, then, was always related to available opportunity and not to any pre-existent 'capitalist spirit'. In the same way, one might invest in Castilian government bonds (*juros*) rather than in commerce or agriculture not because one was anti-capitalist but simply because the rate of return was higher. It is significant that at the end of the sixteenth century, when *juros* gave a 7 per cent interest, money flowed into them; but by the late seventeenth, when the rate was down to 5 per cent, money was diverted back into land. The search for status, both then and now, was a normal aspiration for someone who had money but little rank to go with it. Though in some parts of the peninsula those with new status felt that they were required to 'live nobly' there is ample evidence that throughout the early modern period the newly rich managed to combine both rank and business, so that by the early eighteenth century the trade guilds in the great cities were powerful instruments of the merchant bourgeoisie.

Greater use by scholars of comparative disciplines such as sociology and social anthropology [214], has made it clear that despite inevitable variations the experience of Spaniards was not greatly different from that of other Europeans. In the evolution both of class and of culture, the same forces common to western Europe could be shown to have been active in the peninsula. A native mercantile and bourgeois class was active both before and after the discovery of America, working closely with other trading interests, notably the Genoese financiers [215]. Mercantile fortunes were made, and the early capitalist spirit was active. We know, however, that Spanish traders and financiers were always less in number and had fewer resources than foreigners. The biggest investors in Spain's early overseas enterprises were the Italians.

The view that Spaniards were capable of capitalist enterprise, contradicts the traditional picture, popularised by literary scholars who drew their evidence largely from the imaginative literature of the theatre (Lope de Vega) and the novel (the *Lazarillo*, the *Quijote*), according to which Spaniards were so obsessed by the notion of 'honour' that they were unable to progress economically, thereby dooming their nation to backwardness because of a psychological prejudice. Support has sometimes been given to this traditional view of a non-capitalist Spain, by presenting Spaniards as a nation of (according to González de Cellorigo in 1600) 'bewitched beings, living outside the natural order of things'. The phrase is simple rhetoric, and there can be no justification for thinking that Spaniards, alone of all peoples, lived outside a natural, normal, framework of problems. The course of Spain's evolution shows few significant divergences from the experience of other nations in Europe. In any case, as we have mentioned above, beyond the question of competence in business looms the question of available resources in Spain. Unable to benefit substantially from its empire, the country was in a weak position when trying to assume economic leadership in Europe.

Though many peninsular writers continued to sneer at wealth and to praise mediaeval warrior values, a moneyed bourgeoisie, fattened by trade, developed in Spain. The problem, as in other Western countries, is to trace the evolution of this bourgeoisie, which covered its tracks because its only social aspiration was to attain noble rank and because the vicissitudes of trade caused many fortunes to dwindle. Moreover, whereas the 'bourgeoisie' can normally be identified with the urban middle classes, in the Mediterranean the middle class tended to take the form of an urban elite with noble status, so that in practice it was difficult to distinguish between bourgeois and noble. The dependent status of Spain's commercial relations [216], above all, left few opportunities open to the native bourgeois. As in parts of eastern Europe, some nobles were using their resources to enter the market [217]. The clearly secondary role of the Spanish bourgeoisie did not prevent them being strong and influential at a local level, especially in the seaports, as with the elite of 'honoured citizens' (*ciutadans honrats*) in Catalonia [39] and similar groups in Valencia. But their wider commercial links were very fragile, and in late-seventeenth-century Valencia for example only the merchants of foreign origin appear to have had good international contacts.

Problems of honour in a business context were less deep-rooted than is often imagined. Sixteenth-century writers admitted freely that 'large-scale trading' was as honourable a profession as arms or letters, and in 1622 one of the Military Orders opened its ranks to 'merchants'. Controversy over the status of commerce continued well into the eighteenth century [218], as in England and in France, but long before then there was no practical barrier to the social ascent of those who had made fortunes in large-scale or sea-going trade. Prejudice was directed only against small-scale trade and shop keeping. A shift of attitudes did not by itself facilitate the development of a bourgeoisie; that came only during the eighteenth century, with the growth of the economy and the breakdown of the systems of foreign monopoly control.

The negative vision of Spain's bourgeoisie has been exceeded only by the negative vision of its aristocracy, commonly presented as backward and anti-capitalist. It is obvious that the aristocracy was dedicated to traditional values, with an emphasis on the warrior ethic and the primacy of agriculture over trade. Under Ferdinand and Isabella all known accessions to the rank of noble were based on distinction in warfare [219]. But, as in other countries, the recruitment of the noble class into the governing bureaucracy helped to modify the ideals of the noble ethic, and under Philip II writers complained that the pen had now replaced the sword and that the Castilian aristocracy had forgotten how to fight, thanks to the long years of peace during the reign of Charles V. Moreover, the entry of *nouveau-riche* merchants and others into the noble class created a war of ideas, with the older aristocracy insisting that only blood descent was valid while the newcomers argued, consonant with Renaissance ideals, that service to the state, whether in the bureaucracy or in the universities or in warfare, bestowed a more valid title to noble status [220]. Spain – like England and France – continued to be run by its noble elite, but this elite continued constantly to renew itself, and the humble but noble bureaucratic families of an earlier epoch evolved into great dynasties. In a country with such an ample range of noble status, from the humble hidalgo to the great grandee, problems of rank and precedence continued to have extraordinary importance. Most of the great professional corporations that evolved in the early modern period laid down rules that excluded people who were not of 'noble' origin (the criterion often adopted was anti-Semitic, that is, one had to be free – *limpio* – of Jewish origins). The trend towards aristocratisation intensified, as in France and England, with constant social mobility leading to a proliferation in the number of noble titles granted by the state. This 'inflation of honours', though provoked in part by the wish of the crown to raise cash through sales [221], was also a real reflection of the upward progress of the moneyed and landed elite, proving that Spanish society was not fixed into immovable status categories.

The relevance of the notions of 'honour' and 'purity of blood'. The concept of 'honour' was fundamental to the social stability of all pre-industrialized countries. To possess honour meant to possess the respect of others within one's social and status group, to lose honour meant to lose that respect. The theme occupied a large place in the dramatic literature of early modern times, with the result that scholars have tended to study it through its role in the plays of Lope de Vega and Calderón rather than through its role in real life. This has sometimes led to the (unfounded) opinion that Spaniards had a highly exaggerated code of honour. There may have been specifically Spanish variants to the concept, but in all essentials there was no difference from the way other Mediterranean peoples saw the problem [222]. When honour was respected, social norms were being observed and there was peace and stability. On the other hand, an attack on honour meant that a serious conflict or crime had been perpetrated, such as theft, insult, disobedience, bodily injury or sexual violence. All these offences were crimes against the norm, and the issue of honour was indissolubly tied up with observing accepted norms in society [223]. Baroque plays often dealt with the theme of husbands who took extreme steps to punish wifely infidelity and thereby vindicate 'honour', but it has been suggested that their intention was largely dramatic and moralizing, and they did not reflect active norms [224].

If the insult involved in a crime were not promptly remedied, the family or the peer group of the offended person might take up the affront. This could lead to quarrels and feuds that might last for generations and cause serious disturbances [225]. In an age when there were no prisons of confinement, offenders had to be punished in a way that satisfied the honour of everyone involved. For example if a noble had to be executed it had to be done in a way befitting his honour, by decapitation rather than by hanging, the method used for people of lower social origin. Spain had no police system or public security authority, so the due observance of 'honour' was a fundamental weapon in the fight against crime.

Another common error made about Spanish ideals in the Golden Age, is the claim that society was obsessed by the need for 'purity of blood'. The claim is wholly untrue, since concern for such purity was rare in most of Spain, and taken seriously only in the city of Toledo and a couple more in the south of the peninsula, where there were substantial urban elites of converso origin. Since at least the middle of the fifteenth century, political rivals of the conversos in these cities tried to exclude them from office and demanded the presentation of genealogical proofs of 'purity' from Jewish blood. An important controversy on the theme of anti-Semitism ensued [197]. The attempt to demand 'purity' was widely denounced and completely failed in practice. A study of the Toledo political elite concludes that there was virtually 'no local institution that did not include conversos, despite statutes dedicated to keeping them out' [226]. One hundred years later, in 1547, a last-ditch attempt was made by the archbishop in Toledo to renew the demand for proofs of 'purity'. The demand was denounced by the city of Toledo and by the king's council, and also failed. Private institutions (such as orders of nobility, and the Inquisition itself) continued to exercise the right to discriminate against people of Jewish origin, but 'purity of blood' was never widely practised in Spain or attained legal approval [227]. The system of proofs was expressly denounced in the writings of every significant theologian and legal authority of the Golden Age. In subsequent decades there were constant references to the concept of 'purity' in documents both in Spain and in Spanish America, but they usually reflected residual (and, of course, persistent) anti-Semitism rather than any significant obsession.

Were women disadvantaged in society? Spanish scholars in the last decade have begun to pay attention to questions affecting family life and sexuality [228]. However, in contrast to the numerous studies that have been done for women in English society limited research has been done on the role of women in the Golden Age, so that approximately half the population of Spain remains very much unstudied [229]. Research on the theme has tended to explore three main avenues: women as seen in fictional writing and in literature of the period [230], their activities in religious life

[231], and the way they fulfilled certain social roles (wives, courtesans). Above all, for lack of any suitable historical personages a great number of literary studies have concentrated on the person of St Teresa of Avila, thereby giving her perhaps an undue role as the prototype Spanish woman. One outstanding study has made the effort to show us St Teresa within the context of the real world in which she lived [232]. Fictional writing of that period, as in the short stories of the seventeenth-century Aragonese writer María de Zayas, is probably the least reliable of the three, because it is uncertain to what extent literary references reflected social reality. It cannot be doubted, of course, that fiction can offer valuable insights into several aspects of the question [233]. Non-fiction is not necessarily more reliable. The many books of moral instruction written by clergy of the Counter-Reformation tended to appeal to a desirable norm rather than to the reality of their time. When Cristóbal Acosta affirmed (1585) that the duty of a man was to 'honour woman and never speak ill of her; employ the eyes in looking on her, the hands in serving her, the property in giving her gifts, the heart in making her happy', we cannot be sure that he was describing what men really did or what they should have done. The clergy tried to make sure that men and women shared proper roles within the institution of marriage. Outside the domestic sphere, however, women were notoriously disadvantaged.

Woman's principal role was in the family. Juan Luis Vives wrote a pioneering treatise on marriage (1523), and many Spanish clergy after him devoted treatises to the theme. For the majority of women the norm was matrimony, but there were many exceptions. For example, in northwest Spain at least 16 per cent of women remained celibate [234]. In practice, the presence of single women in a community was often much higher than this, because of factors such as the high number of widows and the entry of girls into convents. At any given moment, nearly half the women under 50 years old might not be in a state of matrimony.

Both Church and state aimed to strengthen the patriarchal authority of the father, with particular concern for the protection of family property. But they also ceased to tolerate the power over life and limb that husbands had once exercised over wives and children; and 'divorces' or legal separations were granted by state and Church courts when the wife could prove systematic beating. The majority of petitions for separation in Spain cited marital violence as the reason. There were two principal grounds for granting separation in a Catholic country, if we go by the practice in Catalonia [180; p. 310]. First, if either spouse threatened the life and honour of the other (a wife from Sitges stated in 1660 that 'she is mistreated by her husband who threatens to kill her and beats her with his fists and kicks her'). Second, if the spouse refused to give economic support (the same wife stated that 'her husband refuses to work and to give her the necessary maintenance'). Impotence (i.e. inability to fulfil marital duties) tended to be cited not in pleas for separation but in pleas for nullity. Impotence was difficult to prove on personal evidence alone, and more weight was put on the testimony of the community. In one case in Catalonia in 1596 the parish priest testified on behalf of the wife that 'he has heard people say many times in the village that the husband didn't have much of a member'.

'It is no surprise', a Spanish priest observed in 1588, 'that in our time there is such unhappiness in marriages'; another the following year commented that 'it is a disgrace to see how openly and unashamedly so many adulteries are committed'. The fact is that in traditional Europe the marriage bond was not always seen as indissoluble [235]. Like any other secular contract, marriage could be annulled if certain conditions, such as the payment of a dowry, were not complied with. Because the contract carried no commitment to permanence, many felt themselves free to break the bonds by mutually agreed separation or even by bigamy. In rural Catalonia, the incidence of separation, apparently accepted by communities, was so high that the bishops placed it at the top of their list of moral failings among the people. In the same period, the offence of bigamy constituted 5 per cent of all the cases prosecuted in Spain by the Inquisition.

The preparation for marriage obliged all women, rich and poor, to acquire some experience with which they could bring benefit to the family household. It was normal for women to do work in the house, and also frequently out in the field. The process started from the early years, when rural families sent their daughters away from home, to spend a number of years in life-cycle service in the towns. The female presence in the urban labour market was always important. Since life-cycle workers had the specific intention of serving for only a short while, until they had saved money (for their dowry) or learned a trade, there was a rapid turnover in their numbers. In the city of Cuenca over one-third of servants left their jobs annually, and a further one-sixth changed their dwellings every year [142; p. 90]. In global terms, country girls employed in domestic service in the towns were a significant long-term feature of the labour market. The high proportion of girls in such employment contributed to the gender imbalance in many European cities.

Women played a fundamental role in the local economy. Excluded from most professional activities by the guilds, they were an essential part of the agrarian economy, not only in the tasks of planting, weeding and harvesting, but also in transporting produce and in buying. At every social level, whether managers of farms or field labourers, whether as dairy-farmers or as keepers of animals, their role was extremely complex and is difficult to define in statistical terms. In some peasant societies, they worked side by side with men. In the Basque lands women played an important role in agriculture. In the Mediterranean area, on the other hand, they appear to have been discouraged from working in the fields, as this was held to endanger the man's honour. Only men, it was felt, could direct the agrarian economy. Even so, a Catalan writer (1617) reflected the classic male attitude in claiming that 'the woman has to be the first to start work and the last to leave off, the first to get up from the bed and the last to lie down in it' [180; p. 334].

It was commonly recognised at the time that woman's role as mother was the most trying of her several duties. It began with the mortal risk of childbirth. In the upper elites, where it was important to produce a male heir to take over the family property, women were under constant pressure to give birth. The pleasure of becoming a mother was superseded by the obligation to beget (male) heirs. At a time when giving birth was still both painful and a risk to life (both of mother and of child), aristocratic and royal wives complied with their duty and ran the risk. The need to produce live births was of course a result of the very high rate of infant mortality, in which possibly one of every three children died in infancy. Elite wives had to remedy the default, particularly if they kept on producing girls and were unable to achieve the desired goal of a male heir. The young (and subsequently notorious) princess of Eboli, who consummated her marriage with the prince of that name in 1557 when she was 17, produced ten births over the subsequent dozen years. She was hardy enough to survive.

By contrast, three of the four wives of Philip II of Spain died as a consequence of childbirth complications, and the king's second daughter Catalina died young of the same cause. The proportion of women dying in childbirth in Spain is not known, but data for other countries show that up to one in five female deaths occurred when giving birth.

Women had an unexpected role in the Church. Spanish villages continued to accept the need for parish priests to take 'house-keeper' mistresses, in part because they felt that the women contributed a practical experience to the often sheltered world of celibate men. In Barcelona in 1561–62 the vicar general issued 57 warnings to clergy of the diocese over their concubines, and in 1613 the Inquisition in the same city disciplined 38 of its clergy for the same offence. A Catalan priest went so far as to affirm in 1539 that 'clergy may in good conscience marry [he meant "cohabit"] even if they are priests'. The staunchly male-orientated Church of the period after Trent marginalised women in some respects but in others firmly recognised that women had a key role. Women's guilds were the mainstay of several aspects of church activity. Above all, women were the majority of churchgoers. In the Mediterranean countryside, the men stayed outside the church, playing at dice and waiting for their women to come out.

The priority given to an all-male priesthood may have prejudiced the previously significant role of females in the religious life of the community. The Church after Trent also tried to minimise the part of women in religious services. Religious reforms brought order into the chaotic world of convents, but enforcement of the strict cloister may have excluded women from a public spiritual role. Against this, however, must be set the major contribution made by the many new female religious orders, as well as by individual Catholic women. The supreme achievement was that of Teresa of Avila, whose influence permeated the religious reforms in both Spain and France, and who was subsequently proclaimed patron of her nation.

Spirituality was a route through which women succeeded in affirming their interests and making a very special contribution. This was not wholly surprising. In traditional Europe women had stood out in popular experience as hermits and visionaries, and continued to carry out the role at all social levels. Holy women, such as the *beatas* in Spain, exercised a strong spiritual influence over local communities and even, in exceptional cases, became the privileged advisers of kings. María de Agreda, a nun in a little Aragonese town, was visited by Philip IV of Spain in 1643, and came to exercise a profound influence over the king, advising him on the highest concerns of state. But religious women were symbols of power in their own right as well: many famous convents were governed by influential abbesses and female superiors, and noblewomen played a distinctive role as patrons of religion and of the religious orders. These favourable aspects coexisted in society with the usually unequal position enjoyed by women in family and economic life. The important religious changes of the sixteenth century did little to change the ambiguity of women's role.

Women in traditional society led cloistered lives: when unmarried they were constantly chaperoned and when married their position seldom improved. A sixteenth-century Spanish Jesuit suggested that young women might be taught to read but not to write (to avoid writing notes to lovers). Moreover, they 'should not go out to see other women, should not dance, should not go to public parties, should not drink wine and should not stir from the house' [180; p. 332]. Girls in Spain were often not even allowed to go to mass, a restriction much denounced by some clergy. Though the cloistering of women was most practised in the upper classes, women of all conditions evaded it at every turn, and the participation of girls in public festivities (always criticised by moralists) was one of the delights of social life in the Mediterranean. Despite obstacles, religion offered a route of escape. Women went to church in order to find company, both male and female, and became the mainstay of parish congregations, organisation and festivities.

Like men, women were free to achieve considerable physical mobility. America is a significant example. Of those Spaniards who registered formally as emigrants to the New World from Seville, women constituted no more than 5 per cent prior to 1519, but by the 1550s they were some 16 per cent and in the 1560s they were as many as 28 per cent. Most were single; in the new lands they carved out their own destiny, fighting where necessary alongside the men.

Some elite women were constantly active in public life and politics, which gave them an escape normally reserved for men. At the highest level, the role was based on matriarchy. Ladies such as

María Pacheco, leader of the Comuneros in Toledo in the 1520s, were fulfilling roles created by their family position rather than by the accident of their gender. Even in wholly traditional societies, kinship and matriarchy allowed women to dictate family politics, down as far as the context of the village community. While Philip II of Spain's son-in-law the duke of Savoy was away at the battle-front in the 1590s, his place as chairman of the state council of Savoy was regularly, and with great effectiveness, occupied by his wife Catalina. The number of such women is legion. The women who directed governments, family estates and religious houses were by no means deprived of their gender. Their role-function may have been essentially as males, for public authority was considered to be the preserve of men. But the attendant support given to their role usually emphasised their female gender, notably in the active propaganda created around the person of queen Isabella of Castile. It is important to emphasise, consequently, that the exercise of power by women at every level was widely accepted. There was no permanent male dominance.

Were the nobility idle and only the peasants hardworking? One of the most enduring stereotypes of the Spanish character, to be found in much of the literature of the Golden Age, was the idea that noble Spaniards did not like to work. The stereotype was given added force by modern literary scholars who claimed their texts showed that work was considered 'dishonourable'. This naïve approach has now been discredited, as students of literature align their work with that of historians and sociologists. There can no longer be any doubt that the noble elite played a fair part in the creation of wealth [236]. Although several studies have been done on the evolution of noble fortunes [237], little is known of the public role of the great families [238]. The impressive extent of noble control over the land is now well documented for much of Spain [239], but though there are obviously negative aspects of any social system where wealth is in only a few hands, it is unclear whether this was exclusively harmful. Certainly the naïve image of all nobles as being doomed by their ethic to do no work, must be rejected. Though grandees were necessarily absent from their estates, these were usually carefully managed, were protected from fragmentation by the system of entail (*mayorazgo*), and figured among the country's leading sources of grain and wool, so that their economic role cannot be underestimated [240]. Participation of Spanish nobles in industry and trade was logical, commonplace and did not detract from their status [241]. Survival of the documentation of noble houses has demonstrated the fairly efficient functioning of the great aristocratic estates and their struggle for solvency during the crisis years of the early modern period [242]. By the more tranquil years of the later century, many nobles were triumphing over the crisis; we have the case in Cuidad Real of a knight of Calatrava, Don Gonzalo Muñoz Treviño (1609–70), who accumulated property and land, with an impressive output of wool, grain and wine, and whose neighbours commented on his capitalist mentality: 'he was never seen or known to spend excessively except when it benefited his holdings' [243].

Problems of wealth and poverty in traditional society. At the other end of the social scale, the only progress made towards a study of the mass of the population has been through the modes of survival: birth, death, diet, poverty. The evidence suggests that in Spain standards of living deteriorated in modern times, with the documentation speaking more of emigration and misery than of betterment. Between about 1530 and 1560 the proportion of registered poor in the cities of Castile increased from about 10 per cent of the population to an average of 23 per cent [244]; the figures do not include unregistered poor such as vagabonds. From the 1580s (as in much of western Europe) mass poverty increased and abandoned infants became a serious problem; an explosion of beggars provoked repressive legislation and there were recommendations, from writers such as Cristóbal Pérez de Herrera, for the adoption of a positive policy. Spanish writers of the time tend to give the impression that most beggars in the peninsula were the dregs of other nations; in fact, Spain had its own problems, as the censuses of 1561 and 1597 bear out. The latter census states, for example, that in the town of Arévalo 56 per cent were registered poor. In Spain, unlike some other Western countries, widespread poverty was doomed to become a basic characteristic of underdevelopment. The recent study of Palencia by Marcos Martín gives a solid guide to the lot of Spaniards in one region [245]; other studies have concentrated on the operation of poor relief [246]. There were and are varying opinions over the causes of the poverty. The most frequently cited reason – heavy taxation – may have affected the poor less than we imagine. The registered poor were exempt from direct taxation, and would have been affected only by indirect taxes. When trying to explain the rural crisis, it may be more convincing to look at larger structural factors such as changes in land use and the collapse of rural investment. It is possible, in any case, that inequitable distribution rather than the weight of taxation was what had the most negative effects, and it may be doubted whether Spaniards were any more heavily taxed than other nations.

Picaresque literature [247], however, tended after 1600 to disseminate the image of a Spain steeped in poverty, and foreign travellers helped to perpetuate the picture of a nation of idle nobles and ragged peasants [248]. Political factors, together with the Inquisition, may have helped to increase incomprehension of the situation in the peninsula. Whatever the reason, Dr Johnson was no doubt right to comment of Spain that there was 'no country less known to the rest of Europe'. Not much is known, to be sure, of the interchange of cultural images between the peninsula and the outside world [249]. What cannot be denied is that Spain had never been a rich country, certainly did not become one during its great age of opportunity during the period of empire, and slipped back very easily into its traditional inertia by the end of the Habsburg era.

Social instability in a country can be viewed through the prevalence of crime, a subject that has received little attention [250]. 'Crime' was a relatively normal variant of social behaviour, taking the form principally of violence and of theft, but it does not surface easily in the available documentation. There were few policing bodies, arrests were easier to make in towns than in the countryside, and a large number of offences went wholly unpunished, creating a substantial 'dark figure' of undetected crime. In broad terms, the bulk of cases tried by the courts were offences against persons or against property. The former usually took the form of violence, or the resolution of personal problems through injury; in large measure they were attacks and mutilations provoked by insults, dishonours and brawls. By contrast, crimes against property were less common, and have been seen as typical of a more modern society, where the accumulation of wealth and the growing gap between propertied and propertyless could lead to social conflict.

Violence in all its forms was common. In the region known as the *montes* of Toledo, of the 1988 cases dealt with by courts in the period 1550–1700, over 42 per cent concerned violence in various forms, and only 10 per cent involved petty theft. Evidence for the late seventeenth century in Valencian and Catalan villages shows a similarly high level of violence within the rural community, aggravated by the widespread possession of firearms: in 1676 the viceroy of Catalonia deplored 'the many great and enormous crimes perpetrated in the principality'.

Coercive violence was often seen as acceptable because it was used as a mechanism to regulate social relations, protect personal and public honour, and control misdemeanours. In such an environment, some violence would not be seen as crime. In the same way, when offences against persons and property were committed by those who controlled power, namely the nobility, they were not prosecuted. Many offences that did not occur in the public domain, such as violence between persons and within the family, did not arrive in court. Prosecution through the courts can in some measure be seen as exceptional; it was certainly more common for rural communities to seek other solutions for offences. There were also many 'crimes' that did not fall within the jurisdiction of the governing authority, since Spain was a mass of conflicting jurisdictions, with state, Church and noble courts sometimes overlapping in authority (for example, the offence of witchcraft might be subject to either a Church or a local or a royal court, or to all three). Since law officials were few and normally non-resident, rural communities were often left to police themselves. This meant that, for lack of law enforcement machinery, many 'crimes' were never punished or prosecuted, and apparently tranquil communities may well have experienced more lawlessness than the records show. On the other hand, in certain rural areas community controls were exercised over offences that may not have been formal 'crimes' but that threatened to disturb social order. In the province of Santander in northern Spain this form of social discipline and policing was the predominant one in the pre-industrial period [251].

A possibly moderate level of crime in the countryside must be contrasted with the situation in the large towns, where problems of housing, food and employment were severe. In 1578 the municipality of Valladolid had to appoint two extra law officers to deal with the increase in theft and murder. For Madrid the reports present a frightening picture. 'Not a day passes but people are found killed or wounded by brigands or soldiers; houses burgled; young girls and widows weeping because they have been assaulted and robbed', writes a witness in 1639. 'From Christmas till now', writes another in June 1658, 'there have been over 150 deaths and no one has been punished'. An analysis of Madrid crime in the late seventeenth century gives some support to these accounts. In 1693, one of the peak years for violence in the period, repeated street-brawls led to the arrest of over 300 persons for disturbing public order; there were 29 recorded murders and 14 cases of rape. The municipal police were unafraid to act against nobility, who that year were implicated in incidents of assault, rape, brawling, theft, wife beating and murder. The authorities initiated 382 criminal prosecutions during the year but 212 of these could not be proceeded with because the accused had fled the city. Over the period 1665–1700 crimes of violence represented about half of all detected crimes, sexual incidents came next (rape, sex-crimes and marriage quarrels), and cases of theft last of all [252].

7 Conclusion

The distinctive features of Spain's historical experience – the centuries of coexistence with Islam and Judaism, the fortunate discovery of a stupendous New World, the sudden inheritance of universal empire – might mislead us into searching for a unique explanation of its subsequent evolution. Like Don Quixote in his search for the fabulous, scholars have often looked for the exclusive ingredient that makes Spain different, and in the process have created an image woven out of the dreams of Spaniards themselves. 'When in ancient or modern times', exclaimed a sixteenth-century conquistador of Peru, Francisco de Jérez, 'have there been such great enterprises of so few against so many, through so many lofty climates and vast seas and endless lands, to conquer the unseen and unknown? Who can equal those of Spain'?

The meteoric rise to world status of 'those of Spain' – 'los de España' – seemed miraculous only because writers then and later invented a scenario in which all the achievements were the work of Spaniards alone (and above all, Castilians). They felt that God had given half the world to them as a reward for their heroism. In the nineteenth century a prime minister, the historian Emilio Castelar, proclaimed: 'Spain created America just like God created the world: America will be Spanish forever!' When affairs began to go wrong, commentators began to search for explanations and scapegoats. Out of this dramatic vision of history was born the concept of 'decline', which Spanish historians such as the conservative politician Cánovas del Castillo fostered in the nineteenth century as an explanation for the failures of their own country, and which was seized upon and used by non-Spanish historians down to the 1960s. The failures of the age of empire produced much introspective pessimism, but the same vein of complaint always recurred, generation after generation. 'Everything is ruined in this country, there is no

87

government, no army, no navy; everything is a fiction, everything is in decline.' Phrases similar to this could be found in writings around the year 1700, but the words were in fact written in a prominent Madrid newspaper in 1901. Around the same date the writer Ortega y Gasset was explaining that 'everything that has happened in Spain since 1580 is decline and disintegration' [253]. In order to criticise the painful present through which they were living, Spaniards attempted to create a successful past, a mythology that yearned for the legendary centuries of success, when the Reconquest had expelled the Arabs, when Ferdinand and Isabella had (they said) united Spain, when Cortés and Pizarro had single-handedly subdued the American continent, and when Spanish civilisation had (as they saw it) dominated the globe.

The so-called Golden Age was in consequence the reflection of an ideology that has prevailed down to our own day. The concept of 'decline' both reinforced Castilian pride in a mythical age of success, and tried to identify the roots of failure in factors – the Inquisition, foreign capitalists, bad kings, subversive Jews – over which Castilians claimed to have little control. Anti-clericals blamed decline on the Church, and went on first to deprive the Church of its property (in the 1850s) then to attack clergy (1936). Clericalists blamed the situation on anti-clericals, Protestants and Communists. The attempt to find an answer to the country's troubles in a lost Golden Age turned out to be unproductive. Spain's problems were in reality inherent in the country's society, economy and ideology. Recent research leaves us with the unsurprising image of a poor nation that was given every opportunity to benefit from leadership of an empire it had never had to conquer, but which lost that opportunity: it is the how and why of this predicament that continues to attract controversy. The will to succeed is probably not in doubt: Spaniards proved to be good soldiers, competent administrators and adequate traders. If they fell behind in any of these spheres they received solid support from Italians, Flemings and the other peoples of the empire. Nonetheless, almost from the beginning there were clear signs that Spain's experience was not going to duplicate the achievements of the Roman Empire. Although leader of a world monarchy, Spain relied overwhelmingly on foreign money, foreign troops and foreign ships to sustain that leadership, an inverted situation to be found in no other empire in history. Coloniser of the American continent, it almost from the first ceased to be able to control the political and economic destiny of the New World. Commercial crossroads of the West, it failed to reap the benefits of that trade and became a colony for European merchants. Recipient of the gold and silver of the Indies, its population began to experience, and for generations, the pangs of poverty. Inevitably, seventeenth-century writers came to judge the whole imperial experience as a tragic mistake, and we can see with hindsight that the Golden Age, if it existed, was there for the few but not for the many. Even the application of the term 'golden' to culture may raise doubts: imperialism promoted the Castilian language and Castilian culture, but at the cost of the Arabic, Catalan and other traditions of the peninsula. Moreover, the impact on Europe was fleeting, and it is significant that the image it most successfully projected on to the rest of the world in the early seventeenth century was an ambivalent one, the delusions of a Don Quixote, the vagabond escapism of a Guzmán de Alfarache.

Many nineteenth-century Spaniards rejected the Golden Age and condemned it as a period of tyranny, bigotry and racism. Was it therefore only a delusion? The answer to that question depends on one's political and moral views, on one's personal consciousness of the identity of Spain, and on the perspective one takes of history.

Glossary

alumbrados – Illuminists, groups of mystics who minimised the role of the Church and of ceremonies.

arbitristas – Writers who drew up *arbitrios* or proposals for economic and political reform.

carrera de Indias – The trading voyage to and from America.

censo – Annuity drawn from loans made to individuals or public bodies; there were various types of *censos*.

chancillerías – Term applied to the Castilian high courts in Valladolid and Granada.

ciutadans honrats – (in Catalan), *ciudadanos honrados* (in Castilian). Honoured citizens, the highest civic rank, equal to nobility, granted by major towns in the Crown of Aragon, especially Barcelona.

Comunidades – The urban 'communities' of Castile, especially those who took part in the revolts of 1520; the persons taking part were *Comuneros*.

concejo abierto – 'Open council', the governing body of many towns and villages in Spain.

conversos – Term applied particularly to Christianised Jews.

corregidores – Crown-appointed civil governors in main Castilian towns.

Cortes – Political assemblies of the realms of Spain.

Diputación – Standing committee of the Cortes, with members appointed from each estate. In Barcelona the *Diputación* (in Catalan, *Diputació*) was also called the *Generalitat*.

fueros – Local laws and privileges, applied especially to the non-Castilian parts of Spain.

hidalgo – One having the status of nobility (*hidalguía*), but without denoting rank.

juros – Annuities paid out of state income for loans to the crown.

letrados – University graduate in law, basis of the state bureaucracy.

limpieza de sangre – 'Purity of blood', freedom from taint of Jewish blood.

mayorazgo – Entail, settlement restricting the alienation of or succession to a noble estate.

Mesta – Castilian guild of sheep-owners.

pecheros – Commoners, tax-payers.

regidor – Town councillor.

servicios – A 'service' or grant of taxes made by the Castilian Cortes.

valido – Chief minister or 'favourite' in royal government.

Select Bibliography

Introduction

[1] Richard Herr, 'American historical writing on early modern Spain', *Society for Spanish and Portuguese Historical Studies Bulletin*, vol. XXVIII (2003) 1–2.

[2] Notably his masterpiece *The Mediterranean and the Mediterranean World in the Age of Philip II*, 2 vols (London, 1972).

[3] The best-known study of Pierre Vilar, is *La Catalogne dans l'Espagne moderne. Recherches sur les fondements économiques des structures nationales*, 3 vols (Paris, 1962). His brief *Histoire de l'Espagne* (Paris, 1958), achieved wide circulation in Spain. For an assessment of his influence on Spanish scholarship, see Roberto Fernández, ed., *España en et siglo XVIII. Homenaje a Pierre Vilar* (Barcelona, 1985), with contributions from fifteen historians.

[4] Henry Kamen, *Spain 1469–1714: a Society of Conflict*, 3rd edn (London, 2005).

[5] John Lynch, *Spain 1516–1598. From Nation State to World Empire* (Oxford, 1991); and *The Hispanic World in Crisis and Change 1598–1700* (Oxford, 1992).

[6] Stanley G. Payne, *A History of Spain and Portugal*, 2 vols (Madison 1973) (e-book).

[7] The textbook by J. H. Elliott, *Imperial Spain* (London, 1963), has never been revised and is outdated.

[8] http://www.isu.edu/~owenjack/spemp/spemp.html

Absolute Monarchy in Spain

[9] There is no detailed study of 'absolutism' in Spain, but the article on Castile by I. A. A. Thompson, 'Absolutism in Castile', reprinted in his essential volume *Crown and Cortes. Government, Institutions and Representation in Early Modern Castile* (Aldershot, 1993), sorts out confusions.

[10] The most recent survey of the reign is by John Edwards, *The Spain of the Catholic Monarchs 1474–1520* (Oxford, 2000). A useful earlier

study is that by J. N. Hillgarth, *The Spanish Kingdoms, 1250–1516,* 2 vols (Oxford, 1978), vol. 2.

[11] The latest short biography of the queen is by Alfredo Alvar Ezquerra, *Isabel la Católica* (Madrid, 2002).

[12] See the important and fundamental study by Teofilo Ruiz on 'Unsacred monarchy. The kings of Castile in the late Middle Ages', reprinted in his *The City and the Realm: Burgos and Castile 1080–1492* (Aldershot, 1992), chap. XIII.

[13] The care taken at their deaths could still be complex: see the rituals for Philip II in Carlos M. Eire, *From Madrid to Purgatory. The Art and Craft of Dying in Sixteenth-Century Spain* (Cambridge, 1995).

[14] Francisco Tomás y Valiente, *Manual de Historia del Derecho Español* (Madrid, 1979), part iv.

[15] J. H. Elliott, 'A Europe of composite monarchies', *Past and Present,* 137 (Nov. 1992), 48–71, deals with the case of Spain. Prof. Conrad Russell has identified the union between Scotland and England as similar to that between Castile and Aragon.

[16] J. Vicens Vives, 'The administrative structure of the state in the six-teenth and seventeenth centuries', in Henry J. Cohn, ed., *Government in Reformation Europe 1520–1560* (London, 1971).

[17] José Antonio Maravall, *Estado Moderno y Mentalidad Social, siglos XV a XVII,* 2 vols (Madrid, 1972); and his 'The origins of the modern State', *Journal of World History,* VI (1961). For the eighteenth cen-tury, see P. Molas, 'La historia social de la administración española. Balance y perspectivas para el siglo XVIII', *Cuadernos de Investigación Histórica,* 6 (1982) 151–68.

[18] José Antonio Escudero, *Los secretarios de Estado y de Despacho, 1474–1724,* 4 vols (Madrid, 1976). On the Council of State, see now Feliciano Barrios, *El Consejo de Estado de la monarquía española, 1521–1812* (Madrid, 1984).

[19] Richard L. Kagan, *Students and Society in Early Modern Spain* (Baltimore, 1974) (e-book). Among recent studies of the higher education system, see L. E. Rodríguez-San Pedro Bezares, *La Universidad Salmantina del Barroco, 1598–1625,* 3 vols (Salamanca, 1986).

[20] Jean-Marc Pelorson, *Les 'letrados': juristes castillans sous Philippe III* (Poitiers, 1980); I. A. A. Thompson, 'The rule of the law in early modern Castile', *European History Quarterly,* 14 (1984); also in [9].

[21] Janine Fayard, *Les membres du Conseil de Castille à l'époque moderne (1621–1746)* (Paris–Geneva, 1979).

[22] Marvin Lunenfeld, *Keepers of the City. The Corregidores of Isabella of Castile (1474–1504)* (Cambridge, 1987), is the latest study of the cor-regidors. Benjamin González Alonso, *El corregidor castellano (1348–1808)* (Madrid, 1970) gives a general survey, supplemented by his *Sobre et Estado y la Administración de la Corona de Castilla en et Antiguo Régimen* (Madrid, 1981).

[23]   Henry Kamen, *Crisis and Change in Early Modern Spain* (Aldershot, 1993), chapter on 'The establishment of intendants in early Bourbon Spain'.

[24]   Hayward Keniston, *Francisco de los Cobos, secretary of the emperor Charles V* (Pittsburgh, 1960). On Charles' key adviser Gattinara, see John M. Headley, *The Emperor and his Chancellor* (Cambridge, 1983).

[25]   Gregorio Marañón, *Antonio Pérez, 'Spanish Traitor'* (London, 1954).

[26]   Francisco Tomás y Valiente, *Los validos en la monarquía española del siglo XVII* (Madrid, 1963).

[27]   Antonio Feros, *Kingship and Favoritism in the Reign of Philip III* (Cambridge, 2000), is the most recent study of Lerma.

[28]   Patrick Williams, 'Philip III and the restoration of Spanish government, 1598–1603', *English Historical Review*, 88 (1973).

[29]   Geoffrey Parker in his *Philip II* (Boston, 1978; repr. Chicago, 2002) holds the king directly responsible for all the problems of his reign. He suggests that the portrait in my *Philip of Spain* (New Haven and London, 1997) is of a king 'who could do no wrong', because I share Braudel's view that Philip II was in some measure controlled by events rather than a controller of events.

[30]   J. H. Elliott, *The Count–Duke of Olivares* (New Haven and London, 1986).

[31]   R. A. Stradling, *Philip IV and the Government of Spain, 1621–1665* (Cambridge, 1988).

[32]   Jesús Lalinde Abadía, 'El sistema normativo navarro', *Anuario de Historia del Derecho Español*, 40 (1970) 85–108.

[33]   The administrative independence of the northern provinces may be seen for example by consulting E. J. de Labayru, *Historia General del Señorío de Bizcaya*, 6 vols (Bilbao–Madrid, 1895–1901); Gregorio Monreal, *Las instituciones públicas del señorío de Vizcaya* (Bilbao, 1974); E. Fernández Villamil, *Juntas del Reino de Galicia*, 3 vols (Madrid, 1962).

[34]   On these three regions, there are revealing essays by I. A. A. Thompson, X. Gil, and J. Casey, in R. L. Kagan and G. Parker, eds, *Spain, Europe and the Atlantic World* (Cambridge, 1995).

[35]   J. H. Elliott, *The Revolt of the Catalans: A Study in the Decline of Spain, 1598–1640* (Cambridge, 1963).

[36]   I. A. A. Thompson, *War and Government in Habsburg Spain 1560–1620* (London, 1976).

[37]   James Casey, *Early Modern Spain. A Social History* (London, 1999), chap. 6; J. M. Bernardo Aries and E. Martínez Ruiz, eds, *El municipio en la España Moderna* (Cordoba, 1996); José I. Fortea Pérez, ed., *Imágenes de la diversidad: el mundo urbano en la Corona de Castilla (siglos XVI–XVIII)* (Santander, 1997).

[38]   *Les Elites locales et l'Etat dans l'Espagne moderne du XVIe au XIXe siècle*, ed. M. Lambert-Gorges (Paris, 1993). For Castile there is a good introduction by J. M. de Bernardo Ares, 'El gobierno del Rey y del Reino. La lucha por el poder desde la perspective municipal' in *La Administración municipal en la Edad Moderna* (Cadiz, 1999).

[39] James Amelang, *Honored Citizens of Barcelona: Patrician Culture and Class Relations, 1490–1714* (Princeton, 1986) (e-book).

[40] Mauro Hernández, *A la sombra de la corona: Poder local y oligarquía urbana (Madrid, 1606–1806)* (Madrid, 1995).

[41] Antonio Álvarez-Ossorio, 'Neoforalismo y Nueva Planta. El gobierno provincial de la monarquía de Carlos II en Europa', in J. Alcalá-Zamora and E. Belenguer, *Calderón de la Barca y la España del Barroco* (Madrid, 2001), 1061–89.

[42] Carmelo Lisón Tolosana, *Belmonte de los Caballeros. Anthropology and History in an Aragonese Community* (Princeton, 1983), is a re-edition of a study of 1966. The work of Julio Caro Baroja, *Razas, pueblos y linajes* (Madrid, 1957) is also fundamental.

[43] Cf. John B. Owens, *Rebelión, Monarquía y Oligarquía Murciana en la época de Carlos V* (Murcia, 1980).

[44] Helen Nader, *Liberty in Absolutist Spain. The Habsburg Sale of Towns 1516–1700* (Baltimore, 1991).

[45] M. A. Ladero Quesada, 'Les finances royales de Castille à la veille des temps modernes', *Annales ESC*, 25(iii)(1970).

[46] Ramón Carande, *Carlos V y sus banqueros*, 3 vols 2nd edn (Madrid, 1965–67).

[47] Miguel Artola, *La Hacienda del Antiguo Régimen* (Madrid, 1982).

[48] Margarita Cuartas Rivero, 'La venta de oficios públicos en et siglo XVI', *Actas del IV Symposium de Historia de la Administration* (Madrid, 1983) 225–60; also her 'La venta de oficios públicos en Castilla-León en et siglo XVI', *Hispania*, XLIV (158)(1984) 495–516.

[49] *Antonio Dominguez Ortiz*, 'La venta de cargos y oficios públicos en Castilla y sus consecuencias económicas y sociales', *Anuario de Historia Económica y Social*, 3 (1970).

[50] I. A. A. Thompson, 'Crown and Cortes in Castile, 1590–1665', *Parliaments, Estates and Representation*, II(i)(June 1982) 29–45; reprinted in [9]. See also Charles Jago, 'Habsburg absolutism and the Cortes of Castile', *American Historical Review*, 86 (2) (April 1981); and his 'Philip II and the Cortes of 1576', *Past and Present*, 109 (1985).

[51] J. I. Fortea Pérez, *Monarquía y Cortes en la Corona de Castilla: Las ciudades ante la política fiscal de Felipe II* (Fuensaldaña, 1990). For the eastern provinces, there is a good outline in English by Xavier Gil, 'Parliamentary life in the Crown of Aragon', *Journal of Early Modern History*, 6 (iv) 2002.

[52] One small example: in a well-known Spanish seaside resort today (2004) there are 10 000 dwellings already constructed illegally but with unofficial permission, and 30 000 others being constructed illegally but awaiting the unofficial permission.

[53] Jean Vilar, *Literatura y economía: la figura satírica del arbitrista en et Siglo de Oro* (Madrid, 1973).

[54] Richard L. Kagan, *Lucrecia's Dreams: Politics and Prophecy in Sixteenth-Century Spain* (Berkeley, 1990).

[55] Cf. J. A. Fernández Santamaría, *Reason of State and Statecraft in Spanish Political Thought, 1595–1640* (New York, 1983). Also his

earlier *The State, War and Peace: Spanish Political Thought in the Renaissance, 1516–1559* (Cambridge, 1977).

[56] Cited by Luciano Pereña in his edition of Francisco Suárez, *De juramento fidelitatis*, 2 vols (Madrid, 1979).

[57] Jean Vilar, 'Formes et tendances de l'opposition sous Olivares: Lisón y Biedma, *Defensor de la Patria'*, *Mélanges de la Casa de Velázquez*, 7 (1971) 263–294.

[58] Joseph Pérez, *La révolution des 'Comunidades' de Castille (1520–1521)* (Bordeaux, 1970); J. A. Maravall, *Las Comunidades de Castilla: una primera revolución moderna* (Madrid, 1979); Stephen Haliczer, *The Comuneros of Castile. The Forging of a Revolution, 1475–1521* (Madison, 1981).

[59] J. I. Gutiérrez Nieto, *Las comunidades como movimiento antiseñorial* (Barcelona, 1973).

[60] Sebastián García Martinez, *Bandolerismo, piratería y control de moriscos en Valencia durante et reinado de Felipe II* (Valencia, 1977).

[61] A. Dominguez Ortiz, *Alteraciones andaluzas* (Madrid, 1973).

[62] H. Kamen, 'A forgotten insurrection of the seventeenth century: the Catalan peasant rising of 1688', *Journal of Modern History*, 49 (1977), reprinted in [23]; for the 1693 rising, S. García Martinez, 'En torno a los problemas del campo en el sur del reino de Valencia', *VIII Congreso de Historia de la Corona de Aragón*, vol. iv, 215–234.

[63] P. L. Lorenzo Cadarso, *Los conflictos populares en Castilla (siglos XVI–XVII)* (Madrid, 1996).

[64] Xavier Torres, *Nyerros i cadells: bàndols i bandolerisme a la Catalunya moderna (1590–1640)* (Barcelona, 1993).

[65] Ruth Mackay, *The Limits of Royal Authority. Resistance and Obedience in Seventeenth-Century Castile* (Cambridge, 1999).

[66] José Sanabre, *La action de Francia en Cataluña en la pugna por la hegemonía en Europa, 1648–1659* (Barcelona, 1956).

[67] Jordi Vidal Pla, *Guerra dels segadors i crisi social. Els exiliats filipistes (1640–1652)* (Barcelona, 1984).

[68] Fernando Sánchez Marcos, *Cataluña y et Gobierno central tras la Guerra de los Segadores 1652–1679* (Barcelona, 1983).

[69] Pierre Vilar, *Le 'Manual de la Companya Nova' de Gibraltar, 1709–1723* (Paris, 1962).

[70] J. M. Torras i Ribé, 'Reflexions sobre l'actitud dels pobles i estaments catalans durant la guerra de Successió', *Pedralbes*, 1 (1981) 187–209; See also Nuria Sales, *Els botiflers, 1705–1714* (Barcelona, 1981).

[71] The best general survey of early eighteenth-century Spain is by John Lynch, *Bourbon Spain 1700–1808* (Oxford, 1989). The standard study in Spanish is A. Dominguez Ortiz, *Sociedad y Estado en et siglo XVIII español* (Barcelona, 1976).

[72] On the reign of Philip V, see Henry Kamen, *Philip V of Spain. The King Who Ruled Twice* (New Haven and London, 2001).

The Making and Unmaking of Empire

[73] Julián Juderías, *La Leyenda Negra* (Madrid, 1914), republished very often afterwards.

[74] Sverker Arnoldsson, *La Leyenda Negra: estudios sobre sus orígenes* (Göteborg, 1960); W. S. Maltby, *The Black Legend in England* (Durham, N.C., 1971). A recent general perspective in R. García-Cárcel, *La Leyenda Negra. Historia y opinión* (Madrid, 1992).

[75] Ricardo del Arco y Garay, *La idea de imperio en la política y la literatura españolas* (Madrid, 1944).

[76] Felipe Fernández-Armesto, *The Canary Islands After the Conquest* (Oxford, 1982).

[77] John M. Headley, 'The Habsburg world empire and the revival of Ghibellinism', in David Armitage, *Theories of Empire, 1450–1800* (Aldershot, 1998) 66.

[78] Anthony Pagden, *Lords of all the World. Ideologies of Empire in Spain, Britain and France, c.1500–c.1800* (New Haven and London, 1995).

[79] Geoffrey Parker, *The Grand Strategy of Philip II* (New Haven and London, 1998).

[80] What follows is drawn largely from Henry Kamen, *Spain's Road to Empire. The Making of a World Power 1492–1763* (London, 2002) (in the USA, *Empire. How Spain Became a World Power 1492–1763* (New York, 2003)).

[81] John Lynch, *Spain 1516–1598. From Nation State to World Empire* (Oxford, 1991) 212.

[82] Haring, Clarence H., *Trade and Navigation between Spain and the Indies in the Time of the Hapsburgs* (Boston, 1918) 199.

[83] René Quatrefages, 'Etat et armée en Espagne au début des temps modernes', *Mélanges de la Casa de Velázquez*, xvii (1981) 85–103.

[84] Geoffrey Parker, *The Army of Flanders and the Spanish Road, 1567–1659* (Cambridge, 1972); *Spain and the Netherlands* (London, 1979), figure 4, p. 28.

[85] Felipe Ruiz Martín, 'Los hombres de negocios genoveses de España durante el siglo XVI', in Hermann Kellenbenz, ed., *Fremde Kaufleute auf der iberischen Halbinsel* (Cologne, 1970) 85.

[86] Felipe Ruiz Martín, 'Gastos ocasionados por la guerra: repercusiones en España', in V. Barbagli Bagnoli, ed., *Domanda e Consumi. Livelli e strutture (secoli XIII–XVIII)* (Florence, 1978). Other aspects of finance are studied by Modesto Ulloa, *La Hacienda Real de Castilla en et reinado de Felipe II*, 2nd edn (Madrid, 1977); F. Ruiz Martín, 'Las finanzas españolas durante et reinado de Felipe II', *Cuadernos de Historia, anexos de la revista 'Hispania'*, 2 (1968); also his 'La banca en España hasta 1782', in *El Banca de España. Una historia económica* (Madrid, 1970); Antonio Dominguez Ortiz, *Política y Hacienda de Felipe IV* (Madrid, 1960).

[87] C. J. Hernando Sánchez, *Castilla y Nápoles en el siglo XVI. El virrey Pedro de Toledo. Linaje, estado y cultura (1532–1553)* (Salamanca,

1994), is a good study of perhaps the most outstanding of Spain's viceroys.

[88] Antonio Calabria, *The Cost of Empire. The Finances of the Kingdom of Naples in the Time of Spanish Rule* (Cambridge, 1991).

[89] G. Parker and I. A. A. Thompson, 'The battle of Lepanto 1571: the costs of victory', in I. A. A. Thompson, *War and Society in Habsburg Spain* (Aldershot, 1992).

[90] Chapter Three of Jan Glete, *War and the State in Early Modern Europe. Spain, the Dutch Republic and Sweden as Fiscal-Military States, 1500–1660* (London, 2002).

[91] David C. Goodman, *Power and Penury: Government, Technology and Science in Philip II's Spain* (Cambridge, 1988).

[92] Aspects of the navy are discussed in J. F. Guilmartin, *Gunpowder and Galleys. Changing Technology and Mediterranean Warfare at Sea in the Sixteenth Century* (Cambridge, 1974).

[93] Henry Kamen, *The War of Succession in Spain 1700–1715* (London, 1969).

[94] David C. Goodman, *Spanish Naval Power, 1589–1665* (Cambridge, 1997); C. R. Phillips, *Six Galleons for the King of Spain: Imperial Defense in the Early Seventeenth Century* (Baltimore, 1986); Stradling, R. A. Stradling, *The Armada of Flanders. Spanish Maritime Policy and European War, 1568–1668* (Cambridge, 1992).

[95] José Alcalá Zamora, *Historia de una empresa siderúrgica española: los altos hornos de Liérganes y La Cavada, 1622–1834* (Santander, 1974); a general survey in V. Vázquez de Prada, 'La industria siderúrgica en España (1500–1650)', in H. Kellenbenz, ed., *Schwerpunkte der Eisengewinnung und Eisenverarbeitung in Europa, 1500–1650* (Cologne, 1974).

[96] Giuseppe Galasso, *Alla periferia dell'Impero. Il Regno di Napoli nel periodo spagnolo (secoli XVI–XVII)* (Turin, 1994); Giuseppe Galasso and Luigi Migliorini, *L'Italia moderna e l'unità nazionale* (Turin, 1998).

[97] Miguel Angel Ochoa Brun, *Historia de la diplomacia española*, 6 vols (Madrid, 1999).

[98] Garrett Mattingly, *Renaissance Diplomacy* (London, 1955).

[99] De Lamar Jensen, *Diplomacy and Dogmatism* (Cambridge, MA., 1964).

[100] M. van Durme, *El cardenal Granvela (1517–1586). Imperio y revolución bajo Carlos V y Felipe II* (Barcelona, 1957).

[101] Friedrich Edelmayer, *Söldner und Pensionäre. Das Netzwerk Philipps II im Heiligen Römischen Reich* (Vienna, 2002).

[102] Paul C. Allen, *Philip III and the Pax Hispanica, 1598–1621* (New Haven, 2000).

[103] J. H. Elliott, *The Count-Duke of Olivares* (Yale University Press, 1986) is largely dedicated to foreign policy. For interesting aspects of secret diplomacy in this period, see M. A. Echevarria Bacigalupe, *La diplomacia secreta en Flandes, 1598–1643* (Leioa, Vizcaya 1984).

[104] William S. Maltby, *Alba. A Biography of Fernando Alvarez de Toledo, Third Duke of Alba 1507–1582* (University of California, 1983).

A recent short study of Alba is Henry Kamen, *The Duke of Alba* (New Haven and London, 2004).

[105]   J. A. Maravall, *La oposición política bajo los Austrias* (Barcelona, 1972).

[106]   See [103]; the earlier essay by H. R. Trevor-Roper, 'Spain and Europe, 1598–1621', in *The New Cambridge Modern History*, vol. vi, *The Decline of Spain and the Thirty Years War* (Cambridge, 1970) is still stimulating.

[107]   Peter Brightwell, 'The Spanish origins of the Thirty Years War', *European Studies Review*, 9 (1979) 409–31.

[108]   José Alcalá-Zamora y Queipo de Llano, *España, Flandes y el mar del norte, 1618–1639* (Barcelona, 1975). An earlier article by the same author is 'Velas y cañones en la política septentrional de Felipe II', *Jerónimo Zurita. Cuadernos de Historia* (1970–71) 23–24.

[109]   Jonathan Israel, *Conflicts of Empires. Spain, the Low Countries and the Struggle for World Supremacy 1585–1713* (London, 1997); and his 'A conflict of empires: Spain and the Netherlands, 1618–1648', *Past and Present*, 76 (1977) 34–74.

[110]   R. A. Stradling, *Europe and the Decline of Spain: A Study of the Spanish System, 1580–1720* (London, 1981).

[111]   Manuel Herrero Sánchez, *El acercamiento hispano-neerlandés (1648–1678)* (Madrid, 2000).

[112]   Hugo de Schepper, 'La organización de las finanzas públicas en los Países Bajos reales, 1480–1700. Una reseña', *Cuadernos de Investigación Histórica*, 8 (Madrid, 1984) 7–34.

[113]   John L. Motley, *The Rise of the Dutch Republic*, published in the nineteenth century in several editions, but now conveniently available as an e-book.

[114]   Geoffrey Parker, *Spain and the Netherlands 1559–1659* (London, 1979).

[115]   C. H. Carter, 'Belgian "autonomy" under the Archdukes, 1598–1621', *Journal of Modern History*, xxxvi (1964); Paul Janssens, 'L'échec des tentatives de soulèvement aux Pays-Bas sous Philippe IV (1621–1665)', *Revue d'Histoire Diplomatique*, 92 (1978) 110–29.

[116]   Rosario Villari, *La rivolta antispagnola a Napoli. Le origini 1586–1647* (Bari, 1967); A. d'Ambrosio, *Masaniello. Rivoluzione e contrarivoluzione nel reame di Napoli (1647–1648)* (Milan, 1962); Giuseppe Galasso, *Napoli doppo Masaniello. Política, cultura, società* (Naples, 1972).

[117]   Luis Ribot, *La monarquía de España y la guerra de Mesina, 1674–1678* (Madrid, 2002).

[118]   R. D. Hussey and J. S. Bromley, 'The Spanish empire under foreign pressures, 1688–1716', in *New Cambridge Modern History*, vol. vi (Cambridge, 1970).

[119]   Alcalá-Zamora, 'Razón de estado y geoestrategia en la política italiana de Carlos II', *Boletín de la Real Academia de la Historia* (1976) 297–358.

Did Spain Decline?

[120]   Pedro Saínz Rodríguez, *La evolución de las ideas sobre la decadencia española* (Madrid, 1962), with a useful bibliography.
[121]   Earl J. Hamilton, 'The decline of Spain', *Economic History Review*, viii (1937–38) 168–79; repr. in E. M. Carus-Wilson, ed., *Essays in Economic History*, 3 vols (London, 1954–62), i, 215–26.
[122]   J. H. Elliott, 'The Decline of Spain', *Past and Present*, 20 (Nov. 1961), repr. in T. H. Aston, ed., *Crisis in Europe, 1560–1660* (London, 1965).
[123]   J. H. Elliott, 'Self-perception and decline in early seventeenth-century Spain', *Past and Present*, 74 (1977).
[124]   Henry Kamen, 'The Decline of Spain: a historical myth?', *Past and Present*, 81 (Nov. 1978), reprinted in [23].
[125]   James Casey, 'Spain: a failed transition', in Peter Clark, ed., *The European Crisis of the 1590s* (London, 1985). An attempt to make population responsible for everything that went wrong in the peninsula ('the model that best explains the economy of early modern Spain is a Malthusian one') can be found in Carla Rahn Phillips, 'Time and Duration: A Model for the Economy of Early Modern Spain', *American Historical Review* (Sept. 1987).
[126]   J. K. J. Thomson, *Decline in History. The European Experience* (Oxford, 1998), in particular chap. 6.
[127]   Earl J. Hamilton, *American Treasure and the Price Revolution in Spain, 1501–1650* (Cambridge, MA., 1934).
[128]   There is an excellent survey of the process by Stanley J. Stein and Barbara H. Stein, *Silver, Trade, and War. Spain and America in the Making of Early Modern Europe* (Baltimore, 2000).
[129]   For re-exports see Artur Attman, *Dutch Enterprise in the World Bullion Trade 1550–1800* (Göteborg, 1983); also his *American Bullion in the European World Trade 1600–1800* (Göteborg, 1986).
[130]   Earl J. Hamilton, *War and Prices in Spain 1651–1800* (Cambridge, MA., 1947), is the standard work on this period.
[131]   Jordi Nadal, *Historia de la población española (siglos XVI–XX)*, 4th edn (Barcelona, 1991).
[132]   Angel García Sanz, *Desarrollo y crisis del Antiguo Régimen en Castilla la Vieja. Economía y Sociedad en tierras de Segovia 1500–1814* (Madrid, 1977); Bartolomé Bennassar, *Valladolid au siècle d'or* (Paris, 1967).
[133]   Enrique Otte, 'Sevilla, plaza bancaria europea en et siglo XVI', in A. Otazu, ed., *Dinero y Crédito (siglos XVI–XIX). Actas del I Coloquio international de historia económia, Madrid-Segovia 1977* (Madrid, 1978).
[134]   Vicente Pérez Moreda, *Las crisis de mortalidad en la España interior (siglos XVI–XIX)* (Madrid, 1980). For the Mediterranean coast, there are data in N. Biraben, *Les Hommes et la peste en France et dans les pays européens et méditerranéens*, 2 vols (Paris, 1975).
[135]   Jordi Nadal, 'La població catalana als segles XVI i XVII', in *Historia de Catalunya*, vol. iv (Barcelona, 1978).

[136]   José Manuel Pérez García, *Un modelo de sociedad rural de Antiguo Régimen en la Galicia costera: la Península del Salnés* (Santiago, 1979). Another recent survey of Galicia is Pegerto Saavedra, *Economía, Política y Sociedad en Galicia: la provincia de Mondoñedo, 1480–1830* (Madrid, 1985).

[137]   David S. Reher, *Town and Country in Preindustrial Spain: Cuenca 1550–1870* (Cambridge, 1990); also his *Perspectives on the Family in Spain* (Oxford, 1997).

[138]   Among the several studies of the 1561 census, see B. Bennassar, 'Economie et société à Ségovie au milieu du XVIe siècle', *Anuario de Historia Económica y Social*, I, i (1968); L. Martz and J. Porres, *Toledo y los toledanos en 1561* (Toledo, 1974).

[139]   Robert Rowland, 'Sistemas matrimoniales en la península ibérica (siglos XVI–XIX): una perspectiva regional', in V. Pérez Moreda and D. S. Reher, eds, *La Demografía Histórica de la Península Ibérica* (Actas de las I Jornadas de Demografía Histórica, Madrid, Dec. 1983) (Madrid, 1986).

[140]   James Casey, *The Kingdom of Valencia in the Seventeenth Century* (Cambridge, 1979). In the useful collection of essays by James Casey *et al.*, *La Familia en la España Mediterránea (siglos XV–XIX)* (Barcelona, 1987), Casey gives a good survey of the family in Andalusia.

[141]   Bartolomé Bennassar, *Recherches sur les grandes épidémies dans le Nord de l'Espagne à la fin du XVIe siècle* (Paris, 1969).

[142]   Quoted in David E. Vassberg, *The Village and the Outside World in Golden Age Castile* (Cambridge, 1996) 70.

[143]   Magnus Mörner, 'Spanish migration to the New World prior to 1810', in F. Chiapelli, ed., *First Images of America. The Impact of the New World on the Old*, 2 vols (Los Angeles and London, 1976), vol. 2, 737–82; the same volume also contains P. Boyd-Bowman, 'Spanish emigrants to the Indies, 1595–98', 723–36. See also the latter's 'Patterns of emigration to the Indies until 1600', *Hispanic American Historical Review*, 56, iv (1976).

[144]   James Casey, 'Moriscos and the depopulation of Valencia', *Past and Present*, 50 (1971); and his 'La situación económica de la nobleza valenciana en vísperas de la expulsión de los Moriscos', in *Homenaje al Dr D. Juan Reglà*, 2 vols (Valencia, 1975), I, 515–25.

[145]   Angel Rodríguez Sánchez, *Cáceres: población y comportamientos demográficos en et siglo XVI* (Cáceres, 1977).

[146]   J. López Salazar and M. Martín Galán, 'Producción de cereales en Toledo, 1463–1690', *Cuadernos de Historia Moderna y Contemporánea* (Madrid), II (1981). The trend was similar in Andalusia: see Pierre Ponsot, 'La dîme, source d'histoire rurale et urbaine', *Actas II Coloquios Historia de Andalucia, Nov. 1980. Andalucia Moderna, tomo I* (Córdoba, 1983) 353–62.

[147]   Baudilio Barreiro, 'La introducción de nuevos cultivos y la evolución de la ganadería en Asturias durante la Edad Moderna', *Congreso de Historia Rural. Siglos XV–XIX* (Madrid, 1984) 287–318;

J. M. Pérez García, 'Aproximación al estudio de la penetración del maiz en Galicia', in A. Eiras Roel, ed., *La Historia Social de Galicia en sus fuentes de protocolos* (Santiago, 1981) 117–59.

[148]   David E. Vassberg, 'The *tierras baldías*: community property and public lands in 16th century Castile', *Agricultural History*, 48(3)(1974); 'The sale of *tierras baldías* in sixteenth-century Castile', *Journal of Modern History*, 47(4) (1975).

[149]   Gonzalo Anes, 'Tendencias de la producción agrícola en tierras de la Corona de Castilla (siglos XVI–XIX)', *Hacienda Pública Española*, no. 55 (1978) 97–111; Gonzalo Anés, *Las crisis agrarias en la España Moderna* (Madrid, 1970).

[150]   Jesús García Fernández, 'Champs ouverts et champs clôturés en Vieille Castille', *Annales E.S.C.*, 20(4) (1965) 692–718.

[151]   David E. Vassberg, *Land and Society in Golden Age Castile* (Cambridge, 1984).

[152]   Francis Brumont, *La Bureba à l'époque de Philippe II* (New York, 1977); see also his 'La rente de la terre en Rioja occidentale à l'époque moderne', *Mélanges de la Casa de Velázquez*, xvi (1980) 237–72.

[153]   Michael Weisser, *The Peasants of the Montes* (Chicago, 1976).

[154]   Noël Salomon, *La Campagne de Nouvelle Castille à la fin du XVIe siècle d'après les 'Relaciones Topográficas'* (Paris, 1964). There is a Spanish translation of 1973.

[155]   Eva Serra, 'El règim feudal català abans i després de la sentència arbitral de Guadalupe', *Recerques*, 10 (1980). See also the group of essays in the *Revista de Girona*, xxxii (118) (Sept.–Oct. 1986).

[156]   I. A. A. Thompson and B. Yun Casalilla, eds, *The Castilian Crisis of the Seventeenth Century* (Cambridge, 1994).

[157]   The authoritative study is now C. R. Phillips and W. D. Phillips Jr, *Spain's Golden Fleece* (Baltimore 1997), though the old study by Julius Klein, *The Mesta. A Study in Spanish Economic History 1273–1836* (Harvard, 1920), still offers food for thought.

[158]   Paulino Iradiel Murugarren, *Evolución de la industria textil castellana en los siglos XIII–XVI. Factores de desarrollo, organización y costes de la producción manufacturera en Cuenca* (Salamanca, 1974). On the problems of textiles in the subsequent period see J. I. Fortea Pérez, *Córdoba en et siglo XVI: las bases demográficas ye económicas de una expansion urbana* (Córdoba, 1981).

[159]   Henri Lapeyre, *Une famille de marchands: les Ruiz. Contribution à l'étude du commerce entre la France et l'Espagne au temps de Philippe II* (Paris, 1955).

[160]   José Gentil da Silva, *En Espagne. Développement économique, subsistance, déclin* (Paris, 1965), has interesting data on the points in the peninsula to which bullion went.

[161]   A. M. Bernal, A. Collantes de Terán and A. García-Baquero, 'Sevilla: de los gremios a la industrialización', *Estudios de Historia Social*, no. 5–6 (1978).

[162]   A. Girard, *Le commerce français à Séville et Cadiz au temps des Habsbourg* (Paris, 1932); J. Everaert, *De internationale en koloniale Handel der Vlaamse Firma's te Cadiz 1670–1700* (Bruges, 1973).

[163]   David R. Ringrose, *Madrid and the Spanish Economy 1560–1850* (University of California, 1983) (e-book).

[164]   Antonio-Miguel Bernal, *La financiación de la Carrera de Indias* (Seville, 1992).

[165]   M. Morineau, *Incroyables gazettes et fabuleux métaux. Les retours des trésors américains d'après les gazettes hollandaises (XVIe–XVIIIe siècles)* (Paris, 1985).

[166]   Henry Kamen, 'The decline of Castile: the last crisis', *Economic History Review*, XVII(i) (1964) 63–76, reprinted in [23].

[167]   P. Molas Ribalta, 'A tres-cents anys del "Fénix de Cataluña". Recuperació i reformisme sota Carles II', *Pedralbes*, 3 (Barcelona, 1983) 147–74.

[168]   P. J. Pla Alberola, *La población del marquesado de Guadalest en et siglo XVII* (Alicante, 1983). For a good survey of the impact of crisis on one community, J. Casey, 'Tierra y Sociedad en Castellon de la Plana, 1608–1702', *Estudis*, 7 (1980) 13–46.

[169]   P. Molas Ribalta, 'La Junta de Comercio de Barcelona', *Anuario de Historia Económica y Social*, 3 (1970) 235–79.

Why was there no Reformation?

[170]   Américo Castro, *The Structure of Spanish History* (Princeton, 1954).

[171]   Claudio Sánchez Albornoz, *España, un enigma histórico*, 2 vols, 2nd edn (Buenos Aires, 1956) available in a very poor English version (Madrid, 1975).

[172]   Elie Kedourie, ed., *Spain and the Jews* (London, 1992), chap. 3: 'The expulsion: purpose and consequence'; Moshe Lazar and Stephen Haliczer, eds, *The Jews of Spain and the Expulsion of 1492* (Lancaster, CA., 1997).

[173]   Henry Kamen, 'The Mediterranean and the Expulsion of Spanish Jews in 1492', *Past and Present* 119 (May 1988); also in [23].

[174]   Benzion Netanyahu, *The Marranos of Spain*, 2nd edn (Ithaca, 1999).

[175]   A thoughtful analysis of the converso problem and the early days of the Inquisition can be found in Gretchen D. Starr-LeBeau, *In the Shadow of the Virgin* (Princeton, 2003).

[176]   Mark D. Meyerson, *The Muslims of Valencia in the Age of Fernando and Isabel* (Berkeley, 1991).

[177]   In English the best, albeit old, survey is still H. C. Lea, *The Moriscos of Spain* (London, 1901). Anwar G. Chejne, *Islam and the West: The Moriscos* (New York, Albany, 1983); Louis Cardaillac, *Morisques et Chrétiens. Un affrontement polémique (1492–1640)* (Paris, 1977); Andrew C. Hess, *The Forgotten Frontier: A History of the Sixteenth-Century Ibero-African Frontier* (Chicago, 1978).

[178] The statistics for the Morisco population were settled by Henri Lapeyre, *La géographie de l'Espagne morisque* (Paris, 1959); the best survey of the whole question is by A. Domínguez Ortiz and B. Vincent, *Historia de los Moriscos* (Madrid, 1978).

[179] Cf. Henry Kamen, on 'Spain', in Bob Scribner, Roy Porter and Mikuláš Teich, *The Reformation in National Context* (Cambridge, 1994).

[180] Henry Kamen, *The Phoenix and the Flame. Catalonia and the Counter Reformation* (New Haven and London, 1993).

[181] Marcel Bataillon, *Erasme et l'Espagne* (Paris, 1937) is the classic work, which tends to give perhaps too optimistic an image of the extent of Erasmus' influence in Spain.

[182] The best modern survey of the spiritual currents of that period is by Alastair Hamilton, *Heresy and Mysticism in Sixteenth-Century Spain: The Alumbrados* (Cambridge, 1992). See also Antonio Marquez, *Los Alumbrados. Orígenes y filosofía (1525–1559)* (Madrid, 1980).

[183] A recent bibliography is Gordon Kinder, *Spanish Protestants and Reformers in the Sixteenth Century* (London, 1983). For some perspectives, J. E. Longhurst, 'Luther in Spain 1520–1540', *Proceedings of the American Philosophical Society*, 103 (1959) 66–93; A. Redondo, 'Luther et l'Espagne de 1520 à 1536', *Mélanges de la Casa de Velázquez*, 1 (1965); Carlos Gilly, *Spanien und der Basler Buchdruck bis 1600* (Basel and Frankfurt, 1985), chap. 5: 'Die Häretiker'.

[184] Among the very few studies on it, three are basic: Kamen [180]; Sara T. Nalle, *God in La Mancha. Religion, Reform and the People of Cuenca 1500–1650* (Baltimore, 1992) (e-book); and Allyson M. Poska, *Regulating the People. The Catholic Reformation in Seventeenth-Century Spain* (Boston, 1998).

[185] The best short survey is by Helen Rawlings, *Church, Religion and Society in Early Modern Spain* (New York, 2002).

[186] Maureen Flynn, *Sacred Charity: Confraternities and Social Welfare in Spain, 1400–1700* (London, 1986).

[187] William A. Christian Jr, *Local Religion in Sixteenth-Century Spain* (Princeton, 1981); *Apparitions in Late Medieval and Renaissance Spain* (Princeton, 1981) (e-book).

[188] J. -P. Dedieu, 'Christianisation in New Castile', in A. J. Cruz and M. E. Perry, *Culture and Control in Counter-Reformation Spain* (Minneapolis, 1992).

[189] C. R. Boxer, *The Church Militant and Iberian Expansion 1440–1770* (Baltimore, 1978).

[190] B. Bennassar, *The Spanish Character: Attitudes and Mentalities from the Sixteenth to the Nineteenth Century*, Trans. Benjamin Keen (Berkeley and Los Angeles, 1979).

[191] H. Kamen, 'Toleration and dissent in sixteenth-century Spain: the alternative tradition', *Sixteenth-Century Journal*, 18(4) (1987); reprinted in [23].

[192] The basic source on witchcraft and the Inquisition is Lea [193], vol. 4. See also G. Henningsen, *The Witches' Advocate. Basque Witchcraft and the Spanish Inquisition* (Nevada, 1981).

[193] The classical history by Henry Charles Lea, *A History of the Inquisition of Spain*, 4 vols (New York, 1906–1908), is now available on-line as an e-book.

[194] The standard general survey by Henry Kamen, *The Spanish Inquisition: A Historical Revision* (New Haven and London, 1998), has a bibliography.

[195] A typical view is that of Haim Beinart, *Conversos on Trial. The Inquisition in Ciudad Real* (Jerusalem, 1981).

[196] Benzion Netanyahu, *The Origins of the Inquisition in Fifteenth-Century Spain* (New York, 1995).

[197] The chapter by J. Contreras in G. Henningsen and J. Tedeschi, eds, *The Inquisition in Early Modern Europe: Studies in Sources and Methods* (De Kalb, Illinois, 1986) has unreliable figures with serious errors.

[198] J. -P. Dedieu, *L'Administration de la Foi. L'Inquisition de Tolède (XVIe–XVIIIe siècle)* (Madrid, 1989) 260.

[199] James B. Given, *Inquisition in Medieval Society. Power: Discipline and Resistance in Languedoc* (Ithaca, 1997).

[200] For some recent social perspectives, Jaime Contreras, *El Santo Oficio de la Inquisición de Galicia* (Madrid, 1982); J. -P. Dedieu, 'The Inquisition and Popular Culture in New Castile', in S. Haliczer, ed., *Inquisition and Society in Early Modern Europe* (London, 1986).

[201] William Monter, *Frontiers of Heresy: The Spanish Inquisition from the Basque Lands to Sicily* (Cambridge, 1990).

[202] See [194], chap. 6: 'The impact on literature and science.'

[203] 'The mechanisms of censorship were of limited significance in altering intellectual development': R. A. Houston, *Literacy in Early Modern Europe. Culture and Education 1500–1800* (London, 1988) 165.

[204] Antonio Márquez, *Literatura e Inquisición en España 1478–1834* (Madrid, 1980) 189–200.

[205] On Spanish culture in Italy, there is a short summary by Franco Meregalli, *Presenza della letteratura spagnola in Italia* (Florence, 1974). See also A. Rochon, ed., *Présence et influence de l'Espagne dans la culture italienne de la renaissance* (Paris, 1978).

[206] For the Netherlands, see e.g. Geoffrey Parker, 'New light on an old theme: Spain and the Netherlands 1550–1650', *European History Quarterly*, 15(2) (April, 1985) 219–37.

[207] Asensio Gutiérrez, *La France et les français dans la littérature espagnole. Un aspect de la xénophobie en Espagne (1598–1665)* (St Etienne, 1977).

[208] Christian Péligry, 'Les éditeurs lyonnais et le marché espagnol aux XVIe et XVIIe siècles', in *Livre et Lecture en Espagne et en France sous l'Ancien Régime. Colloque de la Casa de Velázquez* (Paris, 1981).

[209]   Virgilio Pinto Crespo, *Inquisición y control ideológico en la España del siglo XVI* (Madrid, 1983). One consequence of the controls exercised by the Franco regime in Spain (1939–75), is that Spaniards assume all censorship to be destructive.

Was Spain 'different'?: Society and Culture in the Golden Age

[210]   This does not, of course, detract from the important contribution of Otis H. Green, *Spain and the Western Tradition: The Castilian Mind in Literature from El Cid to Calderón*, 4 vols (Madison, 1963–66).

[211]   J. M. Diez Borque, *Sociología de la comedia española del siglo XVII* (Madrid, 1976); J. A. Maravall, *La Cultura del Barroco* (Madrid, 1975); J. Caro Baroja, *El Carnaval* (Madrid, 1979).

[212]   P. Molas Ribalta, *La burguesía mercantil en la España del Antiguo Régimen* (Madrid, 1985). This has an excellent up to date bibliography. Also José Antonio Maravall in [17].

[213]   William D. Phillips, 'The Castilian community in sixteenth-century Bruges', *Sixteenth-Century Journal*, XVII, 1 (1986). Fundamental is J. A. Goris, *Etudes sur les colonies marchandes méridionales (Portugais, Espagnols, Italiens) à Anvers de 1488 à 1567* (Louvain, 1925).

[214]   The pioneer in anthropological studies was Julio Caro Baroja; a highly influential study is Julian Pitt-Rivers, *The People of the Sierra*, 2nd edn (Chicago, 1971).

[215]   On Spanish–Italian trade, Felipe Ruiz Martín, *Lettres marchandes échangées entre Florence et Medina del Campo* (Paris, 1965).

[216]   For the meaning of 'dependence', see [126], chap. 6.

[217]   Paul Hiltpold, 'Noble status and urban privilege: Burgos 1572', *Sixteenth-Century Journal*, XII(4)(1981) 21–44.

[218]   W. Callahan, *Honor, Commerce and Industry in Eighteenth-Century Spain* (Boston, 1972).

[219]   Marie-Claude Gerbert, in [240]. For the military orders, L. P. Wright, 'The military orders in sixteenth- and seventeenth-century Spanish society', *Past and Present*, 43 (1969).

[220]   I. A. A. Thompson, 'Neo-noble nobility: concepts of *hidalguía* in early modern Castile', *European History Quarterly*, 15 (1985) 379–406, also in [91].

[221]   I. A. A. Thompson, 'The purchase of nobility in Castile, 1552–1700', *Journal of European Economic History*, 8(ii) (1979), also in [91].

[222]   Peristiany, J. G., ed., *Honour and Shame: The Values of Mediterranean Society* (London, 1965).

[223]   Maravall, J. A., *Poder, honor y elites en el siglo XVII* (Madrid, 1979).

[224]   C. A. Jones, 'Honor in Spanish Golden Age drama: its relation to real life and morals', *Bulletin of Hispanic Studies*, 35, 1958. See also Melveena McKendrick, 'Honour/vengeance in the Spanish comedia', *Modern Language Review*, 79 (1989).

[225]   Good examples in [37], chap. 8, 'Obedience to the law'.

[226]   Linda Martz, *A network of converso families in early modern Toledo* (Ann Arbor, 2003) 405.

[227]   Henry Kamen, 'A crisis of conscience in Golden Age Spain: the Inquisition against Limpieza de Sangre', in [23].

[228]   F. Vázquez García, 'Historia de la sexualidad en España: problemas metodológicos y estado de la cuestión', *Hispania*, 194 (Madrid, 1996); Pablo Pérez García, 'La criminalización de la sexualidad en la España Moderna', en *Furor et Rabies. Violencia, conflicto y marginación en la Edad Moderna*, ed. José I. Fortea *et al.* (Santander, 2002).

[229]   *Nuevas perspectivas sobre la mujer. Actas de las primeras jornadas de investigación interdisciplinaria, Seminario de Estudios de la Mujer* (Madrid, 1982).

[230]   Beth Miller, ed., *Women in Hispanic Literature* (Berkeley, 1983); Magdalena S. Sánchez and Alain Saint-Saens, eds, *Spanish Women in the Golden Age: Images and Realities* (Westport, CT, 1996).

[231]   *Religiosidad femenina: Expectativas y realidades, S. VIII–XVIII*, eds, Angela Muñoz and María del Mar Graña Cid (Madrid, 1991); *Women in the Inquisition: Spain and the New World*, ed. Mary E. Giles (Baltimore, 1998).

[232]   Jodi Bilinkoff, *The Avila of Saint Teresa: Religious Reform in a Sixteenth–Century City* (Ithaca, 1989).

[233]   Augustin Redondo, ed., *Images de la femme en Espagne aux XVIe et XVIIe siècle. Des traditions aux renouvellements et à l'émergence d'images nouvelles* (Paris, 1994).

[234]   José Manuel Pérez García, *Un modelo de sociedad rural de Antiguo Régimen en la Galicia costera: la Península del Salnés* (Santiago, 1979) 119.

[235]   P. Ariès, 'The indissoluble marriage', in Philippe Ariès and André Bejin, *Western Sexuality* (Oxford, 1985).

[236]   Cf. Antonio Domínguez Ortiz, *La sociedad española en el siglo XVII*, 2 vols (Madrid, 1963, 1970).

[237]   Ignacio Atienza Hernández, *Aristocracia, poder y riqueza en la España moderna: la Casa de Osuna siglos XV–XIX* (Madrid, 1987).

[238]   The great Mendoza family is an exception; see Helen Nader, *The Mendoza Family in the Spanish Renaissance* (New Brunswick, 1979) (e-book).

[239]   For jurisdictions in Castile, see Miguel Artola, ed., *La España del Antiguo Régimen: Salamanca* (Salamanca, 1966); *Castilla la Vieja* (1967); *Castilla la Nueva y Extremadura* (1971). For *señoríos*, Salvador Moxó, 'Los señoríos. En torno a una problemática para et estudio del régimen señorial', *Hispania*, 94 (1964).

[240]   Marie-Claude Gerbert, *La noblesse de Castille. Étude sur ses structures sociales en Extrémadure de 1454 à 1516* (Paris, 1979).

[241]   Ruth Pike, *Aristocrats and Traders: Sevillian Society in the Sixteenth Century* (Ithaca, N.Y., 1972) (e-book).

[242]   Helen Nader, 'Noble income in sixteenth century Castile: the case of the Marquises of Mondéjar', *Economic History Review*, XXX (1977) 411–28; C. Jago, 'The crisis of the Aristocracy in seventeenth-century Castile', *Past and Present*, 84 (1979). For the evolution of noble rents in Catalonia, see Montserrat Durán, 'L'evolució de l'ingrés senyorial a Catalunya (1500–1799)', *Recerques*, 17 (1985) 7–42.

[243]   J. López-Salazar Pérez, 'Una empresa agraria capitalista en la Castilla del XVII: la Hacienda de D. Gonzalo Muñoz Treviño de Loaisa', *Hispania*, 148 (1981) 355–407.

[244]   Annie Molinié-Bertrand, *Au Siècle d'or. L'Espagne et ses hommes. La Population du royaume de Castille au XVIe siècle* (Paris, 1985).

[245]   Alberto Marcos Martín, *Economía, sociedad, pobreza en Castilla: Palencia 1500–1814*, 2 vols (Palencia, 1985). For another perspective, Claude Larquié, 'Une approche quantitative de la pauvreté: les madrilènes et la mort au XVIIe siècle', *Annales de Démographie historique* (1978).

[246]   Linda Martz, *Poverty and Welfare in Habsburg Spain. The Example of Toledo* (Cambridge, 1983). Work done for the poor by confraternities is described by [187]; and by W. J. Callahan, 'Corporate charity in Spain: the Hermandad del Refugio of Madrid, 1618–1814', *Histoire Sociale*, 9 (1976) 159–86.

[247]   J. A. Maravall, *La literatura picaresca desde la historia social* (Madrid, 1986), the last work of a great historian.

[248]   For some English views, see Patricia Shaw Fairman, *España vista por los Ingleses del siglo XVII* (Madrid, 1981).

[249]   J. N. Hillgarth, *The Mirror of Spain, 1500–1700* (Ann Arbor, 2000).

[250]   On some aspects of crime, see R. Pike, 'Crime and punishment in sixteenth-century Spain', *Journal of Economic History*, 3 (1976) 699–904, and Henry Kamen, 'Public authority and popular crime. Banditry in Valencia 1660–1714', *Journal of European Economic History*, 3(iii) (1974) 654–87, reprinted in [23].

[251]   T. A. Mantecón, *Conflictividad y disciplinamiento social en la Cantabria rural del Antiguo Régimen* (Santander, 1997). Teofilo Ruiz, *Spanish Society 1400–1600* (London, 2001), has two short but unsatisfactory chapters on the theme of 'violence'.

[252]   Henry Kamen, *Spain in the Later Seventeenth Century 1665–1700* (London, 1980) 168–9.

Conclusion

[253]   José Ortega y Gasset, *España invertebrada* (Madrid, 1964).

Index

109

Index

Index

Index